FEARMORPHOSIS

FEARMORPHOSIS

MAN IS A FEAR SISYPHUS BEING WATCHED BY PANOPTICONS

Desh Subba

Library of Congress Control Number: 2023914250
ISBN: Softcover   979-8-3694-9280-2
                eBook   979-8-3694-9279-6

To order additional copies of this book, contact:
Xlibris
AU TFN: 1 800 844 927 (Toll Free inside Australia)
AU Local: (02) 8310 8187 (+61 2 8310 8187 from outside Australia)
www.Xlibris.com.au
Orders@Xlibris.com.au
854668

AUTHOR

DESH SUBBA, was born in the rural district of the eastern part of
Nepal in 1965. He is a founder of Philosophy of Fearism and Trans
Philosophism, what he calls "two eyes" or perspectives on interpretation
and critical analysis. And now his third eye project is Fearmorphosis.
He and others following his earlier works have published books,
journal articles and popular magazine pieces on these topics as well
there are interviews on video. His essential writings and thinking
are challenging to present and past philosophers. From the two eyes,
Subba looks at philosophy, language, morality, politics, economics,
and the environment. It is a natural approach he takes with a Fearism
vision differing from classical, modern, postmodern, and Marxism.
He proposes that the world, meaning-making and life can be seen
better from these eyes or lenses. His ideas continue to influence many
contemporary philosophers, professionals, students and authors.
Fearmorphosis is his latest approach to a third eye—it is also known
as higher consciousness and mind-eye in Eastern mythology.

ABOUT THE BOOK

Typically without conscious awareness, we neglect to see that we live in a mythical world largely operating on a vision of segmenting and reductionism, focusing on the smallest particles. Yet, there are other myths too we are influenced by and may influence them to serve our growing consciousness for a good life. For, example, there is Sisyphus, the Panopticon, the Scapegoat, Das Capital, and Metamorphosis as literary and powerful motivational contexts driving humanity.

A person desperate for survival heaves up his life, family, and capital. Meanwhile, they always think they are being watched by the spiritual and physical Panopticons. To reach the mountain-top and subdue their competitors or enemies, they scapegoat innocent people. We see millions of people become refugees, victims, laborers, and disabled by wars, beliefs, egos, needs, desires, and the pursuit of happiness. Yet, progress is not so easy, it is even ironic. Not only in our escaping we scapegoated ourselves but humans also scapegoated Nature. Driven by a recurrence of fear-based ways and stories, Heavenly Earth became Hell by our doing. It is time to see fear for its major role. It is time to excavate and rewrite history, culture, morality, politics, literature, and philosophy through a systematic criticism of Sisyphus, the Panopticon, and the Scapegoat point of view. This book is the foundation for it. Among a number of analytical perspectives, it focuses on classic existential literary teaching stories, like Metamorphosis, The Myth of Sisyphus, and No Exit from a new Fearmorphosis lens.

CONTENTS

PART FOUR

PART FIVE

EDITOR'S COMMENTARY

Fear is the power of all power. -Desh Subba

In reality, fear is a terminator. It terminates other emotions. To look from a fearism point of view is fearmorphosis. -Desh Subba [1]

Desh Subba's major books, from *Philosophy of Fearism* (2014), *Trans Philosophism* (2021) to now *Fearmorphosis* (2023) are stretches of our imagination and thinking, led by a unique Nepali-born man and writer. He bridges the East and West in his work; he flaunts and dances on the page in wildness and then in strict logic; he poets, invents games and allegories, writes short plays and theorizes. He keeps readers on their toes.

I've been fortunate to have edited several of his works and have co-written a few books and articles with him since 2015. In terms of what I would like you to know about the process of my editing Subba's work, it is already expressed in detail in Fisher (2021), Editor's Commentary for *Trans Philosophism*, whereby I tell of my challenges as a fluent English speaker interpreting someone where English is not their first language (as is the case with Subba). At one point in that commentary I state "To be a good interpreter, I also have to be willing to learn, and to challenge my own favorite, if not rigid, thought and beliefs." [2] At times, I have left Subba's distinct traditional masculine use of pronouns to dominate the text, and at other times I have taken liberty to update it more for a fluid gendered worldly learner. His style is for some rather off-putting.

Specifically, as I am a long-dedicated fearist thinker, it is not always easy to agree with everything Subba says about fear and reality—but I have to respect he is a long-dedicated fearist as well. And never one to be a 'pleaser' as a philosopher, he is creative and always searching for the next innovation in applying the fearist thinker's lens. This new book is no exception from that imperative of his overall intellectual *oeuvre*.

Indeed, Desh Subba, poet, fiction writer, and most important to him is the skeptical philosopher and iconoclast. In this new book, a sort of third of his trilogy of books on philosophy of Fearism, Subba steps forward in PART ONE – MYTH with what is an intriguing analysis of the myth of Sisyphus. He begins this part of the book by setting out the tone of his own inquiry and also his request for readers, which boils down to wanting us all to see things from multiple (pluralist) perspectives. Even the most cherished things ought to be seen from all angles. He calls us then to look at the nature and role of fear in such an open-minded way. This echoes his own reconstruction of the meaning of Sisyphus, going beyond Albert Camus and the W. cannon of interpretations of this ancient myth. He interweaves his literary criticism skills with Sartre's philosophy and other literary kernels from the existential canon. He says we ought not let the image of Sisyphus and its doctrines and ideologies of what it is symbolic of, dictate our thinking afresh.

Subba challenges in his philosophical and artistic-poetic way, that there may be a hidden way of seeing, a metaphysical yet practice way of interpretation, of the "stone" as focused object and less on the inner life *per se* of Sisyphus the human. Subba tells his version of the myth, relates it to his point of view of fearmorphosis—and, critiques existentialist's fascination with absurdity and meaningless struggle(s) as the best way to understand the human condition. Hint: Subba is classifying the kinds of Sisyphuses that exist and have been written about. I won't give away any more here of Subba's re-interpretation in this commentary, only to prepare you for it. He turns our habitual attention to the other, less noticed. The good artist always does that.

Yet what is this new fearist term Subba presents: fearmorphosis? From beginning to end of reading his manuscript, I continue to explore what it means and what new purpose it serves beyond fearism or trans philosophism? He takes "metamorphosis" seriously as a very interesting word and idea (echoes of Kafka) and then transposes it *via* the fear-prefix technique, something he has done from the beginning of his interest in *fear* as central and ontologically precedent to the human experience—that is, human motivation and shaping of humanity and its relationships to all things. Merriam-Webster: *morphogenetic* - relating to or concerned with the development of normal organic form. So, fearmorphic or fearmorphosis makes total sense to Desh Subba if fear is so important as he says, and that it gives a lot more meaning in real terms to humanity to write the new hybrid term and listen to it be pronounced. That is, it is *more* affectively charged and determinate—it is more provocative in pointing out that metamorphosis is *both* external *and* internal development. Evolution and history, and change and metamorphosis go hand-in-hand; and, *fear* is always there present as the catalyst, as the yeast, and as the metaformic, matrix-like pattern or template for all that is created. Humans have too long ignored this fearological truth about fear, he argues. In his second book, Subba wrote a principle/law of his thought, which is that: "Fear" is best seen "as gravity of society" [3]. One cannot get more foundational in a proposition than that.

At least, that is my initial interpretation as to why Subba goes through this trickery of sorts to tell us to change and adapt to the reality that fear is so morphogenetically and metaformically pregnant with potential—for good and not so good. Fear, says Subba from the beginning of his work, is many things and cannot be over-simply stuck in the binary boxes of only good vs. bad. And especially, his project is to bring fear out of all the "negativism" it carries in history and in most people's minds: "Fearism has a positive perspective towards it" [4].

He offers a philosophy of Fearism, and its new-flavored variants, as a teaching for how to build a better understanding and relationship to fear, from multiple 'eyes' or lenses and a wide-open imaginary of possibilities—across knowledges and disciplines. We have to learn to fly with this term "fear" and attach it, consciously and critically, to many other terms, like metamorphosis, to bring it to life and to bear new fruits. This is why I love this thinker on fear—he is totally unique and brings us a series of gifts to consider.

In PART TWO, Subba, turns from Myth form(ation) as part of civilization processes to inevitably the Morality form(ation); and all the time keeping us aware that these are shaping processes of us and not only are we creating them to conform to our shaping will. There is a dialectic of drive and forces in the shaping, directing and planning of a world—of a reality.

With guarding as his work-a-day professional life, Subba is well-versed on the role of security systems and their paradoxes. He wrote, "In an autocracy, the dictator has more Panopticon vision; people are horrified that their ruler is watching them but the dictator is in more terror than the people." Usually, that's not our common sense understanding.

Our security and insecurity (and fear) experience is not just internal and psychological but is highly sociological. At the root of routes in human behavior, deep below consciousness for the most part, he tells us that fear(ism) is operating overall as the master template shaper. And in Part Two the formation he focuses on is the cultural disciplining function of the Panopticon (e.g., which Foucault and others have analyzed critically). Subba writes in that introduction: "Civilization, and culture tried to develop a just human. According to time, various forms of Panopticons changed. It was a fearological device to bind people in forms of discipline." However, Subba may surprise some readers by not just being a liberal (or anarchist), he sees the conserving essential role of Panopticons to help people be moral and just citizens. Even the philosopher and their theories are of this kind with their own surveillance formations. But he thinks we need to classify types of Panopticons more carefully, understand them better, and also be critical of its excesses and misuses. Panopticon, Sisyphus and Fear travel closely in the same operations of the individual and collective, argues Subba.

Analysis and advice on how to best live is core to Subbaian thought. In rather classic style of writing philosophy and situated in the Eastern communalist traditions, he shies not away from generalizations and rather optimistic universal claims, which may trouble many of his postmodern or more radical critics. For example, he claims: "People are inmates." He means to awaken our deadened senses and habits—he is saying, like Plato and other's before him, we are all sociocultural creatures—and, imprisoned slaves, more or less. But he believes he answers that truth with even greater truths that shall help set us free.

In PART THREE, the fearist author's perceptivity leads into the deep formation of Scapegoat. Not merely a behavior, it has a Super Structure, he points out, like an archetypal form for human existence and it causes so much damage. The finer processes and classifications of scapegoating gets his attention. He shares rituals of sacrifice as a major form of scapegoating and writes brutally: "Divorcees scapegoat their children. The heartless teacher scapegoats students." And when he turns his critical fearist lens on Capitalism, Subba notes: In marketing, one famous slogan is, "Customer is always right." He then links this logically to "God is always right." It is clear for Subba, that even secularist business and elitism has its ideology and religion at its base.

His observations of business and sacrifice come through strong and hit a nerve. He has a business masters degree and work background and works in the security industry of the working classes on the front-line, and thus, he sees things real and raw first-hand. Meanwhile, the philosopher in him cannot avoid critique. One wonders if he sees himself as a willing scape-goat? Nonetheless, he shows us that everyday truth of how humans live generally, is sometimes hard to bear and mostly we forget. Yet, as a public intellectual, Subba is relentless and demanding that humanity face its existential and everyday truths. He assesses reasons for such scapegoating and theorizes, but underneath he sees a common cause not always fully compatible with reason. I'll leave that explanation for readers to uncover from his work, rather than spoil it here.

In PART FOUR we get a good sense of Subba's views of economics but also the interiority of the patterns and dynamics of modern society, under Capitalism. He critiques Marx and others for inadequately observing human behavior and contexts, and he presents his own views. There are strong statements made by the author: for example, "Look! How scary a face we have today.... Let's view the earth, a new world can be seen from the fearmorphosis. It is open. We need to see the world from this tower." This repeated theme of gaining new perspective on the ordinary, on our theories and philosophies, is at heart in everything Subba thinks and writes. The details of taking the new perspective are seemingly less important than us merely getting new perspectives. Subba offers no grand savior to this planet's troubles but he offers us ways to get unstuck and try out new perspectives. However, he wrote, "The fearists have been applying Fearism in philosophy, literature, education, healthcare, criticism, politics, ecology, and linguistics, but usually never apply it re: capital. It is a capital perspective doctrine we ought to challenge. Das Capital has less about capitalism and more about the labourer's crisis. Labourers are human beings. Therefore, better to say human capital. Now, we can see fearmorphosis in Das Capital."

Fearmorphosis, if taken seriously as a rational explanatory synthesis, puts many prized things in the current economy of the globe onto the platform of the irrational. Modernity and its unquestioned assumptions are under attack in this Subbaian move. Although, not an outright postmodernist attack, as that is not Subba's positioning, his fearmorphosis critique says: "Ground-rent so capitalised constitutes the purchase price or value of the land, a category which like the price of labour is *prima facie* irrational." That means they are fear-based and unethical, bottomline. Owning and selling land is an oxymoron. I am particularly in strong agreement, that to turn around this world to a sustainable, healthy and sane condition, including our mind, we have to untangle the irrational from the 'rational' we think we are operating from. That is *radical*. This latter term, however, is not even found in most of Subba's fearism writings.

In *Fearmorphosis*, he actually uses that term only once: "In the forest, many animals live. They have a radical nature." Why use "radical" in this context? There are several reasons, but on the top I believe he does so because he contrasts the sanity of Nature, of which he continually expresses his respect in his philosophy. The natural (non-human-made) laws and principles of a 'good' and 'moral' and 'rational' economy—as way of life—is found intact for us to learn from. Such learning would truly be radical, and indeed that is what ecological scientists and activists and poets and philosophers have been saying for over 70 years in the West, at least. The way humans create "the usurer" and concomitant dominating ways (often irrational) of economics is just too easily accepted and unquestioned for the most part. And thus, Subba would prefer a re-analysis and a fearanalysis to get our human enterprises back on track—to get us to unwind this knot he once called the "fear circle" [5]—another formation of meta-Sisyphus(?). He laments but he doesn't prophesize. Steadfastly, as the philosopher must, Subba writes his next PART of this new book with blunt attack and understanding that things will be very difficult to turn around and step out of the self-reinforcing fear circle, which is leading their current course on the way to mass extinction.

In PART FOUR, with a historical and philosophical critique of Capitalism and Marxism (also found in his book *Trans Philosophism*), and other ideas, Subba shares his basic view of human evolution and economic dynamics, along with his problem of the types of Sisyphuses that emerge in power-labor relations and survivalist conditions. He wrote, "When we observe the exploitation scenario, developed countries are exploiting poor and developing countries. I call it, Net Exploitation because there is nothing gross. The exploitation of industry or capitalism is gross because it is a mixed labor-power, family, and social crisis."

Subba gives an observant synopsis *via* his classification of types of capital, and he also gives types of fear and sacrifices that go with it. The author contends with classical thought: "Marx focused, on money as the power of all powers. I reject it. And it was first rejected by Aristotle. My argument is the power of all power is not money; fear is one step bigger and earlier than it." He also, with dispassion and logic, rejects much of the classical foundations of Communism here. The fearist, Subba, leaves readers the impression he wants to think freshly about labor, power, money and capital in the economic systems offered to date. He challenges ideological radical fervor, or even tradition, or oversimplification and redundant habits of thought in this domain. This makes him one of the most unique fearists in the world to apply his lens to economic theories. Subba states his mission here: "My effort is to find the actual story of Das Capital. To have the best life, we look at multiple options. My dissertation is the synthesis." "Das Capital's name is given by Karl Marx. I saw the embryo of fearmorphosis in its womb."

Fear Sisyphus is another way of describing "Historical Fearism" he notes. And in conclusion, Subba wrote of his limited but pervasive vision for a better world, that "Only a philosopher-ruler is the best to rule a nation as said by Plato, but the best ruler ought to be a fearism philosopher." That may be the case but it is still untried as very few have even heard of a fearism philosopher. However, that is not a fact that deters Subba's project. I can certainly relate to his persistence as my own fearwork has been turtle-slow to catch people's attention.

Then comes a radical artistic shift in the text. But an introduction to it is present just prior, and we know we are readers in the hand of a poetic writer-thinker of great span: Subba concludes: "Between boulder and Sisyphus, exists means of subsistence. When stopping the supply of it, a stone and Sisyphus pauses as the statue of the universe."

PART FIVE is narrative-poetic-play(fulness), on the author's part. Why end such a tome upon this kind of story? No one really knows. The Kafkaian character Gregor Samsa is endlessly referred to throughout most of Subba's *Fearmorphosis*. Perhaps he's the human icon of Fear + Metamorphosis? Readers can make up their own mind. What one reads here is Subba's literary analysis and fearmorphosis hypothesis in action with Kafka's text.

With limited space here, I believe it is best to leave more unsaid than said, and conclude in agreement with Ngan, from a recent review article, that overall:

> Subba's writing is poetic, vivid, and full of energy. The use of cultural and historical stories, tales, and literature, combined with striking imagery is aptly used in his work to combine the intellectually analytical, with the emotionally phenomenological. Stylistically, like the philosophical works of Plato, Descartes, and Hume, you are not being lectured and walked through a precise and rigorous argumentation. [6]

Welcome to this circle tour of evolution, of fear, and of human civilization and its ways, for better or for worse. The Nepali writer-thinker, Desh Subba, is offering to be our confident tour guide in *Fearmorphosis*.

R. Michael Fisher
May 23, 2023
Nanaimo, BC, Canada

End Notes

1. Subba (2021b).
2. Fisher (2021b), p. xix.
3. Subba (2021b), p. 146.
4. Subba (2014), p. 332.
5. Ibid., pp. 111-13.
6. Dylan Ngan. https://phimag.org/blog/trans-philosophism-a-review

PART ONE

MYTH

FEAR SISYPHUS

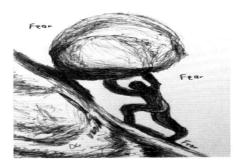

Figure 1 Untitled. Ball point pen drawing by Desh Subba ©2023

Beginning

The myth of Sisyphus is absurd. Camus has written on fear but not to the extent of fearist thinkers, like myself. Fear is central to fearists yet seldom do they use absurd or centralize it in analysis of the human condition; mostly because life isn't absurd or meaningless within a philosophy of Fearism. Life has meaning or is meaningless but that connotation depends on the context of the genesis of meaning made by the observer of human experience and writers of existentialist persuasion. Meaningless is the absurdist's crisis. Not so with the fearists.

I first used *fearmorphosis* in an interview that was done by Bishwa Raj Adhikari in his blog [1]. Hence after, I was enlightened by its importance and began to penance. The central theme of Camus's writing is, "The workman of today works every day in his life on the same tasks, and this fate is no less absurd" [2]. Such an insight doesn't represent large numbers of people. It is a prison and victim idea and itself is imprisoned within the 20-21ˢᵗ-century human mind and its philosophies. Another name for this misleading generalization is: absurd.

I submit that a fearist generalization, is that the human must be free from this particular form of a victim idea and absurd position; however, it is an imperative of freedom based on seeing the human as a fear Sisyphus. "We all properly fear something on a daily basis," philosopher Kasper Renee Johansen writes in validating the philosophy of fearism [3].

Mostly implicitly, fearism was noumena for almost all philosophers. We fearists recently are bringing it to phenomena. In nature, water flows, air blows, and clouds fly. These repeat the same process all the time. Their regular route is zigzag. They are non-living things. We are a man; we have rationale and *fear*.

Fear homes in the brain. Some feeling homes in the mind. We can empirically experience it. The pressure of rock directly hits the amygdala and blinks the fear-fire. Generally, it doesn't have access to the mind. The mind has water of emotions. Most philosophers place fear in the water. Of course, its realm is in heaven, sea, and earth; the kingdom is the brain and mind. General fear comes from the mind but special forms comes from the brain.

We have many myths and stories where a snake and Gods have multiple heads. In the east, Ravan has ten heads. One of the holiest Hindu temples is Pashupati. It lies in Kathmandu, Nepal. There is an idol of Lord Shiva. It has five heads. We can see multiple head Buddhas. Whether East or West we have snakes in the myth that have many heads. The myth of Sisyphus's multiple heads is closed by a single myth. His big head goes absurd. Fearmorphosis excavates them. It can be applicable everywhere as a tool of interpretation, meaning-making and critical analysis.

In philosophy, one world is interpreted by a different philosopher in multiple ways. For example, Parmenides and Pythagoras were a supporter of the disappearance world. Heraclitus was in favour of appearance as truth. Socrates, Sophists, Plato, and many philosophers followed them. Even the Phenomena and Noumena of Kant are not far from it. Such many paradigms are available in philosophy. Some applied in langue and some argue from parole.

The relationship between Sisyphus and the boulder is not simple. Death is at its center.

According to Cubists, Sisyphus can be seen from left, right, up, and down. When we took him from different corners, a single image looks multiple.

According to Leela writing, Lord Krishna was entering the assembly hall of Kansa, and people saw him differently. Founder of Leela Writing, Indra Bahadur Rai writes, "When Lord Krishna entered into the assembly, he was seen from multiple perspectives. Mallas saw him as the strongest male, women beheld him as a statue like lustful, and common people saw him as a diamond and gold-like man, Gopalas saw him as an honest man, the ruled one took him as an agent of giving punishment, Bashudeva and Devaki saw him as an infant, Kangsa took him as a cruel death, Abidushas found him a gigantic and giant figure, the sages saw him as a celestial element, and Brishuies took him as their supporting God (Bhagwat 10/43/17)" [4]. It is a different person's perception. Leela means a play. Lord Krishna appears in various incarnations in the epic Mahabharata. It is called Krishna Leela.

First, Indra Bahadur Rai applied it in a Nepali story Kathputaliko Man (Mind of Puppet). His disciple Krishna Dharabasi applied it in novels by Radha and Sharnarthee (Refugee). Dharabasi collected characters from 21 books and reconstructed them in Sharnarthee. His Radha won a prestigious Madan Purskar Award in 2005 in Nepal.

Some writers followed this technique. In Leela Writing, Rai has taken reference from Jain's philosophy. Leela Writing is popular in Nepalese literature. Dr. Indra Bahadur Rai from India has similar to my design in Leela Writing. It was a Writing Movement in Nepalese literature in the 1970s. The story of Guru Prasad Mainali, Paralko Aago (husband and wife's quarrel is a straw fire. After some time, their quarrel would be terminated) is the original story written by

Mainali. Rai Leelaed (deconstructed) it and argued for many sub-myths like their quarrel metamorphosizes into divorce, killing, suicide, and other activities, etc. This Writing is still followed by his disciples.

Rai and Dharabasi have slight contrast in their writing though both highlighted Leela. Rai has applied a single myth to multiple myths whereas Dharabasi has applied multiple characters to a novel. My approach is just Leela (play), which is demarked between fearleela and non-fearleela.

Dharabasi points out that the cause of the metamorphosis of the body is fear of self-protection [5]. In Jain philosophy, one of the blind men touched the trunk of the elephant and understood it as a banana tree. Another touched the tusk and understood it as a thorn. Another touched the body and understood it as a wall. They understood the elephant differently [6].

Leela and Jain have similarities. We can draw a line between the red and the light golden color of the sunbeam. Between these two dots, a person perceives separate colors. Before non-blinds felt dissimilar about an object, here blinds felt the same object distinct. Perception of blind or non-blind doesn't matter, it varies.

No one attended to the stone, every viewer looked at the cunning Sisyphus. The rock is made marginal and Sisyphus central. I am changing this position. I am putting the rock central and Sisyphus as marginal. Fearmorphosis is my method which focuses on the boulder because it is on the head (Figure 1) and its size is representative of Typhon (e.g., monster, serpentine, of a tremendous voice).

Sisyphus is generic. It and he can be read from myth, proverb, narration, epic, play, story, beliefs, conservation, economics, and value. We look at statues from one place. Any object and belief can be seen as new from another side. We are an options-oriented species; thus, we seek options. The fearmosphosis is the paradigm in this genre. It varies with prior ideas. Deconstruction and metamorphosis don't have a distinct feature as fearmorphosis. Fearmorphosis is the continuation of the Heart Card; it is the process of Playing Cards theory I have written of before [7]. The Playing Cards theory argues that in the state of nature, there were Spade, Diamond, Heart, Club, and more Cards. They denoted emotions. And, the Heart Card represents fear. The society was structured by Heart Cards, which is fearmorphosis. That is, fear is the great shaper morphogenetically (as basis of metamorphosis) of outcomes, of things, of processes, of ways of being.

Is Sisyphus hanging in the myth of a suspension bridge? Is the curse of Sisyphus absurd? Is to wrest up to a mountain-top freight a suicide? Is man's birth on this earth futile? I have written "A man by birth is a fearful animal, and life is the process of fearlessness" [8]. There is nothing futile in that, even if it is challenging to attain.

Can we metamorphosis the metaphor of Sisyphus into an 'allegory of fear'? It is a matter of deep research. 'Metamorphosis: the myth of Sisyphus' is the thesis, antithesis, and fearmorphosis is synthesis. I have five points to argue it;

Giant stone
Water shortage in Ephyra (Corinth)
The tension of Æsopus. (Father of Ægina)
Fear of Zeus (Jupiter), Hades, and Thanatos
Thanatophobia (Fear of dying)

A Sisyphus is a thesis. Every man is fear Sisyphus in one sense. Why does he gaze as antithesis at the hell? He explores and discovers confusion. Misleading life is absurd. He looks at his droste face. Misguidance has multiple ways in the jungle. The guide or trickster takes us to an illusion to clarify it. What the guided finds is a delusion because [s]he walks falsely. They carry a bucket of false ideas and distribute them to society as delicious fruit. People have it and spray the scent everywhere. We are spellbound by such elixir. In Sisyphus and the boulder, the physical picture too easily conceals the hidden metaphysical one.

Assume it is a movie. Sisyphus, stone, mountain, Hades, Thanatos, Zeus, Ægina, and Æsopus roles. Sisyphus is the leading character.

Hades, Thanatos, Zeus, Ægina, and Æsopus are on-site back-drop roles. Look at the poster once before the leap to antithesis.

The movie begins with a man pushing a boulder up a very steep mountainside. A terrible situation is ahead of him. Forgetting all these momentarily, could he think and feel meaningless action? The answer is, 'no'. What was his first feeling and reaction when he heaved up a massive stone? Precisely, his reaction was fear of accident and escape. Almost 95% of people are afraid and seek the best place to find rescue in this critical condition. A man took shelter under its canopy. He could not recall anything except rescue. The heaving-up stone represents pessimistic, tragedy, suffering, anguish, pain, sorrow, tension, anger, sadness, worry, stress, miser, trouble, grief, disappointment, unhappiness, gloom, and frustration but the falling boulder only represents fear (afraid, terror, fright, panic, horror, and alarm).

Steadily ramping up the myth, he becomes a myth of the 'allegory of the fear Sisyphus'. The rock is a head; Hades and Thanatos strike the brain. Fear Sisyphus had three options 1st physical, 2nd semi-physical, and 3rd metaphysical. Metaphysical is a spirit and Panopticon.

The physical body, consciousness, knowledge, and fear come before the rock. In the context of Sisyphus, never comes happiness first. The audience sees 'The Myth of Sisyphus' in Camus's documentary. I am looking at my projector. Camus understood and explained absurdly; but I view it as fearmorphosis.

The stone crushes Sisyphus or Sisyphus crushes the stone? The absurd idea of Camus is practical, or stone of Sisyphus is reasonable? The concept of Camus is a metaphor but what is in real life? On the base of the image, do we look at its absurdity? We escape as fast as we can. We have been running since the beginning of civilization, yet, Pandora's box of fear is chasing us always. We are runners of time and space. Thus, we are 'fear Sisyphus'.

How many metastones are in our life? Did Camus notice it? In The Myth of Sisyphus, we can see our scary faces like in 'The Picture of Dorian Gray'. We are constantly under The Picture of Dorian Gray and try our best to push it away. Why did the stone need selecting as an symbol? Why did not we choose a lotus? Because the lotus cannot carry a Sisyphus meaning. The stone can carry a load better than a flower. Basic human "fear struggle" [9], distinct from Marx's class struggle, is not far beyond what the stone can convey so well.

Once a baby is born, his meaning begins. Sisyphus's freight doesn't appear at birth. It starts with the progress of Empiritionism (Empiricism + Rationalism = Empiritionism) [10].

Infants and the insane are good patterns. They don't know the physical and metaphysical rock. They are innocent and silent. They don't follow the route of the robot man (Sisyphus). How did Sisyphus become a robot? Was he Sisyphus by birth? Fear is a terminator; it made him a robot, and he sought freedom; his process was fearless. How can he be a free man? Cross the myth with two-lines [11].

People are always sandwiched between two stones: fear and fearlessness. There is no option except rescue from being hit by a boulder. If a man is a euthanasia; let the stone roll over him. Mostly it doesn't happen. If it happens, then come to the absurd. Even Sisyphus doesn't sacrifice his life; he runs away. He did it when Thanatos came to take his life. A boulder is his witness. What time rock is above our head, nothing comes to mind apart from preserving life. Rescue is the primary concern; the rests comes as secondary. Hence, we are 'fear Sisyphus.'

We perceive distinctly the same object, fable, and story anchored in our eyes, nose, tongue, skin, and ears (i.e., many senses). On this basis, we can understand Sisyphus in different ways. The celebrity poster of Sisyphus and Boulder is boarding everywhere. In the poster, Sisyphus is under a big rock. Was he interested in pushing it? Was his motivation his desire, need, will, happiness, and is it absurdity? The question comes: what does force him to ram it up? He never desired it. Thanatos and Hades rammed Sisyphus, but who shoves a man, and what is his stone? Vision is in the eye.

The relationship between Sisyphus and the boulder is not simple. Death is at its center. For instance, a car is about to fall on the slope. What will be the first reaction of the passenger-absurd, suffering, suicide, or acceptance? Loud screaming, crying, restless, nervous, faint, shouting, unconscious, trance—and, escape is their first expression. Are these absurd reactions? These are not for absurdity, suicide, or the search for meaning. Do they have time to think and remember assets, relatives, and love? Is it worth it for them? Is meaning itself meaningless or is the universe absurd? Do they accept so easily the accident (to die)? It is not like The Myth of Sisyphus. While a stone is falling; they shout, and beg for help, "help, help... God!". What is the exact expectation of the mourning word? Which emotion is behind it? How to denote this idiom? It is less hypothesis and more realistic.

Regularly we hear such pity words in critical situations. Nobody leaves it simply like the name of useless. They try to escape, rescue, preserve, and protect. People mourn it at the time of earthquakes, tsunamis, cyclones, fire, flooding, landslide, and volcano. These are synonyms for falling rock. Emergent action, response, and rescue are expected. A slight delay can cause death.

Nobody let roll a stone overhead. Several spiritual rocks are in our surroundings. Man must run faster than it. It is a reality. Life must accept it. Acceptance has no alternative. Stone and fear crushed his fate. Stone is external and fear is internal. In this position, it is hard to find room for absurdity and other emotions. When Sisyphus reached the summit, he had the fright of 1st falling from the height, 2nd crushed by a boulder, and 3rd dropping from the next side.

Repetition is not only absurd; it can be behaviour, addiction, and mental crisis that can be looked at from a fearological text. If a person is passionate about football, he always plays. Gamblers, alcoholics, drug addicts, food addicts and even family violators apply it. If someone starts to do violence 1, 2, and 3 times, it becomes their passion and is toxic. The character of an individual always repeats the same action. Nowadays, most people are addicted to mobile phones. An employee first goes to work for income later it becomes his routine. So, he, again and again, repeats the same action. Suppose the manager said, "You stay at home, I give you your salary." It is hard for him to stay at home because he became a workaholic. He is a workaholic as Camus mentioned [12].

The myth of Sisyphus ruled mythical life. Fearmorphosis overrules it and argues practical issues. I categorize various passions. Camus writes, Whether or not one can live with one's passions whether or not one can accept their laws, which is to burn the heart they simultaneously exalt-that is the whole question [13].

MODELS OF SISYPHUS

Generally, people understand and use Sisyphus as Camus said. But there are many people who are untouched by Camusian Sisyphus. Some examples are given below.

Philosophical

A philosophical Sisyphus doesn't go to work every day. Suppose he is an employee. He goes to work for his means of subsistence but his focus would be on philosophy. He wakes up in the morning, takes bath, takes breakfast, and goes to work. Even though his foot is walking, his mind is busy with heaving up ideas. Sometimes he doesn't know where his foot is taking him because his mind is busy solving problems. A very famous example is when Socrates was invited for lunch. On the way, he had a question. He stopped and tried to solve it. It took a long time to sort it out. When he sorted it out and went to lunch, lunch was already over. It happened many times to Albert Einstein, Karl Marx, and some other thinkers. Many artists and musicians come under this category, including Leonardo da Vinci, Michelangelo, Pablo Picasso, Vincent Van Gogh, etc. Philosophers and scientists forget everything when they are handling cases. It gives them ecstatic pleasure to do so. Their delirious expression can be seen in the boulder. What Shangri-La they get from work, they cannot get elsewhere.

Agedness

In society, the number of retired and old citizens is higher than working men. They don't go to work. Most of the time they stay at the home. Gardening, doing exercise, and playing is their daily routine. They are not Camusian Sisyphus; they are aged Sisyphus. Most countries give allowance to them for old age. Allowance, pension, and saving are their financial source. They live in a hospice.

Children

On average, the home has three children and one employee. Students go to schools and universities. Their goal is to succeed in education. To achieve it they study. Student life is beautiful and happy in one sense. Their nostalgia is occupied by it. Everyone recalls it as a Golden Time. They don't push a mythical stone. They carry books and walk towards the hills. In Kafka's novella *The Metamorphosis*, *Gregor Samsa's family, there are four members. Only Gregor works as Sisyphus before the metamorphosis into the insect.

Economical

A businessman does less physical than mental work. He heaves money into the mind. He lives in a luxury home and drives the latest model car but his mind rolls within capital. When they earn more, they feel happy and pleased. At the time of loss, it is similar to a downward turn of the boulder. It depends on what nature of the business he does. It doesn't matter, he shoves a boulder as much as he can.

Politician

A politician lives with politics and thinks with politics. If it is possible, he eats and beds with it too. Politics is his boulder. Many politicians give up their families and devote themselves to party work. I've met many political Sisyphuses who've lost family and property in the name of politics. Such Sisyphuses we can see mostly in developing and poor countries. They are full-time political Sisyphus.

Social

Some people devote their life to the name of social work like Mother Teresa. She was born in Macedonia and spent her entire life in Kolkata. She did social work till the end of her days. Her pleasure and happiness were derived from it. Nobody requested of her a role as social rock. It was her generosity, she enlightened herself. Many such pious social Sisyphuses we can see.

Sport

If we go to see the players like Pele and Maradona; they started to practice when they were a child. Nowadays, for the Olympics and other games, some countries coach players from childhood. Those children's motive is to win gold medals and make the nation proud. The gold medal is their mountain-top, they have to kick their game to the destination. The sport has several parts: traveling, trekking, racing, hunting, fishing, reading, etc. A player always practices and thinks about his game. It is an addiction. Without passion, it is impossible to climb Everest.

Addict

Some people have addictions regarding eating, drinking and other activities of the gambling, smoking, and drugs. From time to time they repeat it and feel uneasy without it. It frequently haunts their mind, and they feel an appetite for it. A gambler losses his assets in gambling, but he cannot give it up. His low self-identity and esteem do not permit him to be a good man.

Social Media

We are dominated within a social media era today. It scapegoats people in the name of facilities. They always look busy with their devices. Working, walking, driving, talking, and eating, they engage with it. Even in the toilets they take their mobiles. Some play games; some see Facebook and WhatsApp. Thousands of entertainment, news, and games are available on this plate forum. A single mobile phone snatched radio, TV, camera, newspaper, music, and theatre. It made people social media Sisyphuses and superseded the restraints of the classical myth.

Mobile

The number of mobile Sisyphuses is rapidly increasing. Twenty years before, very few people were addicted to it. Now, it is rare to find people without it. They are engaged all the time on mobile. They miss many opportunities and effective work tasks because of this addictive craziness. It wastes time and money. The hazardous situation impacts the home, working stations, schools, markets, etc. Neither do they get a punishment for its overuse; nor, it has any relation with work. At some level, this craziness is known by most as absurd but it nonetheless made them mobile Sisyphuses and their underworld thrive. They are self-made Sisyphus models.

Unemployed

A large number of populations come under this category. Some of them are depending on family income, some wander around and some feel lazy to do jobs. How can we apply the Sisyphus metaphor to them? Maybe, they are out of the myth, but we cannot exclude them--because they are part of society. In Gregor Samsa's family, Mr., Mrs., and Grete Samsa didn't go to work. They depended on Gregor's income.

More than half the population of the world is female. In some countries, they are forbidden to do work. They are scapegoated. Biased and prejudicial sources of scapegoat are culture, religion, belief, law, and constitution. Females have been discriminated, tortured, exploited, and dominated.

Miscellaneous

In miscellaneous, there are many people who aren't required to go to work every day. Among them, we can consider the disabled, insane, and infants too. Their life is 'free,' their decisions are more or less free. No one can disturb their liberty. Multiple options are available for them. To maintain their life they are not obligated to push the mythical stone.

The creator of science, technology, invention, creation, and construction does not work as Camusian Sisyphus. Key to their life, they hold themselves. They are self-made Sisyphus but they feel the oppression regardless, of being watched by Panopticons (see Part Two).

Every profession can be Sisyphian but they don't follow the Guru. They disperse in various directions and become a single myth. Homer and Camusian Sisyphus cannot rule them. All Sisyphus(es) have a common point which is fear. We can classify them as fearmorphosis and non-fearmorphosis.

Fearmorphisized are those that are metamorphosed by fear. Every day going to work, earning money, and doing exercises comes under fearmorphosis. Desire, will, pleasure, ego, peace, and hobby passions come under non-fearmorphosis. These are not directly metamorphosed by fear.

STORY OF SISYPHUS

There saw I Sisyphus in infinite moan.
With both hands heaving up a massy stone.
And on his tip-toes racking all his height.
To wrest up to a mountain-top his freight;
When prest to rest it there, his nerves quite spent.
Down rush'd the deadly quarry, the event.
Of all his torture new to raise again;
To which straight set his never-rested pain.
The sweat came gushing out from every pore.
And on his head a standing mist he wore.
Reeking from thence, as if a cloud of dust.
Were raised about it.
Down with these was thrust [14].

Sisyphus was the cunning, king of Ephyra. In Ephyra, there was a shortage of water. One day Sisyphus saw Zeus disguised as an eagle, kidnapped the daughter of Æsopus. Her name was Ægina. Sisyphus witnessed it and he dealt with Æsopus. He told Æsopus "If you give water in my kingdom, I will tell you where Ægina, is". He had no choice. He accepted the deal. Sisyphus told him what he saw. Later Zeus knew that Sisyphus told Æsopus. Thus, he became angry and sent Thanatos to kill him. When Thanatos arrived at Ephyra, Sisyphus wondered. He knew Thanatos came to kill him. He used his smart idea. He tricked him. He said, "I am at the end of my days.

I never thought so early, I die. It is my fate that I got a chance to see a brave death on Earth. Before I die, I want to give you the gift of a jewel. It is my last desire; I want you to wear it." Thanatos was pleased with his honor and agreed to wear it. When he wore it, he enchained himself. It was made to chain slaves. Sisyphus imprisoned Thanatos. Later, Hades knew it and dispatched the god of war to release Thanatos.

In Tartarus, he humbly requested Hades that his wife disrespect him after death. Sisyphus persuaded Hades to return to Earth in order to chastise his wife. Hades agreed to let him go for one day. He cheated death one more time. For many years more he lived facing the curve of the gulf, the sparkling sea, and the smile of the earth [15]. He enjoyed his earthly life. Mercury came and seized the impudent man by the collar and, snatching him from his joys, led him forcefully back to the underworld, where his rock was ready for him [16]. He pushed a stone eternally to the peak.

Sisyphus started his journey during the water crisis. It was his duty to supply water to people. Shortage of water caused the death of citizens. It created a miserable atmosphere. If water cannot give, people cannot drink and farm. It is not just the myth of Sisyphus; it is a fear metaphor too. To protect life, Sisyphus rolled several tricky games. Æsopus 1st, Thanatos 2nd, and Underworld 3rd are in play. What was the reason to cheat?

Panumas King writes in his article on Albert Camus and the problem of absurdity, "the absurd as the futility of a search for meaning in an incomprehensible universe, devoid of God, or meaning. Absurdism arises out of the tension between our desire for order, meaning, and happiness and, on the other hand, the indifferent natural universe's refusal to provide that" [17].

In his opinion, absurdity arises from tension but tension arises from out of what? It is a basic issue of Camus. My understanding differs from his; the majority of tension arises from *dread*. Once we mute it and examine it what result will come? Does consequence come absurd? Is it fit for the cover picture? He showed, one sees merely the whole effort of a body straining to raise the huge stone, to roll it and push it up a slope a hundred times over; one sees the face screwed up, the cheek tight against the stone, the shoulder bracing the clay-covered mass, the foot wedging it, the fresh start with arms outstretched, the whole human security of two earth-clotted hands [18]. The poster speaks it. I am trying to show a 'live show' of the poster. It can be intensely discussed. Before entering discourse; first, examine human life. What percent absurd and nihilistic consists, and what percent fear consists? Is our birth, not a boulder or a universe? Why are we pushing a big stone into this cosmos? When falling down a bus from the steep, what do people feel? It is a matter of factuality. He had several Pandora boxes. It represents his crisis. A crisis is a foundation of stone. To maintain it, he faces brooks crises. In life, we can see a person heaves up his capital. In Camusian words, it can be sealed by his death.

The absurdity idea is unproductive, pessimistic, infinite moan (in Homer's words), and suicidal. A man is productive; he is free to be condemned to such gloom. From the healthy seed, sprouts healthy buds, Plato said. Bud grows a healthy plant. Nihilistic considers out of nothing, nothing is produced. It is also said in Samkhya, what is not cannot be produced. Satkaryavada (Sat means existence and Karya means the manifested effect) is a major principle of Samkhya philosophy. In Karanabhawat (कारणभावात्) it says, the effect has the nature of the cause. My point, out of healthy buds, a healthy plant is produced. Once fear is managed well, it gives a fresh flower in life.

The cunning Sisyphus is past reading. But we hardly notice why he played the cunning one. Everyone knows rescue for life. If he missed using his talent he could be missed from life. When Thanatos was in the chain, jeopardy appeared in the country; no one was dying. While people lived long afterward chaotic problems arose on the Ephyra.

Sisyphus takes advantage of deaths. It is not openly done; the sufferer hardly knows the fact. Suppose, I am an employee; I must be humble, sincere, honest, loyal, and a polite Sisyphus. I must obey the employer's order and rule if I disobey; a need to roll a rock. It is the average life of the employee. To be condemned to it requires protest. It is an individual revolution against individual fear. Its nature is white in dark slate.

Sisyphus is not only Sisyphus; he is a religion, a culture, a myth, and a race. Why did he deceive Thanatos and Hades? He did it for his will to live. Homer writes, Of all his torture new to raise again. He was in thanatophobia. So, he fought death. These were terrible wars. For his cunning, God sentenced him. Sisyphus's opinion, he was right but it was cunning for deaths. In the picture, Sisyphus is pushing a boulder.

Camus explores the absurd and concludes futility. Can we reach his meaning? Does he want to give meaningless meaning? Meaningless is a meaning. How knowledge is formed-entry of raw-fear release product (knowledge). In the morning, we leave the house and return in the evening. We walk under stones. The rock of the house is different, however, it is a stone. The mouth is always open. At any time, the rock opens its devouring mouth and devours us. We cannot rejoice over Sisyphus.

Religion, culture, custom, blind belief, and superstition are based on a *super fear* structure. A piece is thrown, and it is said, don't do this and, that, then disease, sin, law, the curse are born. It attacks the child's slate mind and accepts hell and ghost. The ghost is accepted by the communist manifesto. Even people take it lightly, but it is as messy as the boulder. It is a 'Y' element according to Gerald C Maccallum's concept of liberty. It has many forms. Sisyphus is a hero of the chain. Jean-Paul Sartre cited the waiter's example as bad faith. It is not bad faith; it is mixed with fear and delicious. The waiter believes in it. The state is running a horse and a Jockey is riding on it. If Sisyphus had not been afraid, would he roll the stone?

Terror of not working, not producing a crop, and not making profit is always at the 'On his head a standing mist he wore' (Homer). It is a belief; "You get punished if you don't worship God." Sisyphus rams a stone, the waiter provides service; the manager does managerial work—all have a similarity. God orders Sisyphus, the supervisor orders the waiter, master orders the manager. The head clerk orders

Gregor Samsa. They compel to obey orders—if not, they will heave up and down a massive stone.

The legend was mythical. God commands Sisyphus, but who commands a man? In the end, exploration terminates in fear. Manv is a 'fear Sisyphus.' Camus writes, What need had I of so manv effort [19]? In Hindi and Nepali, we write like मानव (manv). It means human beings. Darkness chases him. Darkness doesn't kill instantly; kills in tortoise moves. Some are his choice; others impose on him. Sisyphus yelled at me and said, "Why don't you see my burden? Why do you search for my meaning? Am I an ambassador of meaningless? Does Meaningless mean fearless? I'm scared. At any moment a stone falls on me. When a stone is in my head, it is not absurd."

Sisyphus was a king. He could order me, but he did not. He could issue a decree, but he did not. I imagined the underworld.

Society used to make stories and read myths. In the myth, Camus condemned life but lifeless is a stone. Sisyphus shoved the stone up to the peak. The world was silent. They were watching a movie.

A man with zero consciousness is a rock. Meaningless life is a boulder too. Why did Sisyphus obey God? When his consciousness awakens and says, "I am not a rock." He opens his eyes. He is not a rock.

What does he see with the first eye, his expression is, "When the body is crushed by the stone, I will die." Why does pleasure, happiness, love, will, desire, sorrow sadness, suicide, pain, and injustice not come to his mind? Why do the country, the people, society, relatives, property, and the Ephyra not come to intelligence?

No one can think of anything until save a life. That can be metamorphosed into 'motivational fear'. Are Gods Sisyphus? Yes, they are. They are God Sisyphus as the capitalist Sisyphus. God shoves punishment, blesses, and saves a life.

The 1st rock, the 2nd death, and the 3rd god are mountains; apart from these, a man had social, political, economic, Hades, and Thanatos. More terrible mountains he might climb afterward. He was in hell. Hell; people had hell consciousness. The outsider's view was different. From time to time; he remembered Typhon. At what time he recalled, he saw the death. The Typhon stone was more significant than the physical. This curse was given to him by God. Whether God or the devil, Typhon was the giant rock.

SISYPHUSES

Politician rolls debate
Capitalist heaves up capital
Labour rams sweat & blood
Philosopher shoves idea
Scientist rolls experiment
Writer drives letters
Mathematician magics numbers
Singer rehearsals voice
The dancer moves hand, and leg.

Most people are Push Sisyphuses except those aged, mad, children, and the sick. Everyone has a deadly quarry in mind; first fear of falling a person, and second fear of falling an object. Therefore, he rams and rams to the peak.

We are not reading Sisyphus; we are reading 'we'. Every manv is a 21st century Sisyphus. Postmodern Sisyphuses are different from classic ones. Did Sisyphus not have hope and desire? His hope and desire were stoned and suppressed by 'fear-man'. He rolled a rock because he hoped one day, he would be free. After being free, he wanted to fulfil his desire and hope. If he had no appetite, how could he be a man? He would be a 'stone man' and his heart be an emotionless 'stone'.

Sisyphus is a paradigm of how will and aspiration end. Why couldn't he choose and apply his decision? He was free but he became a stone, said, Rousseau. His stone is not free; had been standstill for a long time; was walking side by side with living and non-living stones. His decision, choice, and freedom were frozen under the amygdala. Once he recognized these, nobody bound him in a cage, said Isaiah Berlin. He was a freeman. A man is free as a nude kid. Rousseau said, "Man is born free and everywhere he is in the chains." It is true but 90% of the chain is erected by a man and 10% is external.

WHAT IS FEAR SISYPHUS?

Knowledge makes a man; he uses it for freedom and happiness. Freedom is his natural right, but he's too shackled to utilize it. He doesn't begin with man; rather, begins with the amygdala, consciousness, knowledge, and fear. He is his master. Master doesn't have other masters than himself. He is a servant of a master. The servant is not free, but the master is free. Master can enjoy freedom. His freedom is within his territory. He is a Rene Descartes man. My Sisyphus is a 'super fear man,' he penances to bring the *Ganges river.

CAMUSIAN CRISIS

Suicide is a growing case in philosophical court. A man does two kinds of suicide, mental and physical. Physical is guided by mental. Mental is guided by his suicidal tendency. Gregor Samsa did suicide in *Metamorphosis* and *Georg Bendemann attempted in *The Judgment*. It is time for a metamorphosis of Camusian's suicide case.

For any reason, it has no reason to suicide. It is an offense. Does it have a relation with the allegory? Who doesn't roll the stone have more probability of liberty? Many people have a crisis of not being able to eat, enduring humiliation, scorn, prestige loss, failure, tension, competition, inferiority, financial difficulties, torture, and deprivation. The best model we can later see in Mary Anne Walkley's case. World Health Organizaton reported in 2021 every year some 703,000 people complete suicide. Its causes are financial problems, relationship break up or chronic pain and illness, additional reasons are conflict, disaster, violence, abuse, or loss, and a sense of isolation. Do we agree with the report? Did we trace the suicide of Gregor? Pressure, injustice, and oppression can provoke action. Grief and acceptance alone are not the causes. He looks to see hell everywhere, said by Sartre.

A man suffocates by the atmosphere. It terrifies and chokes his throat. In this situation, he can't concentrate on work. He loses patience. Some suffer from pessimism as described by Arthur Schopenhauer. It flows negative currents. Those that lose mental screws, they do it. It is a 'screw loss' or 'suicide haemorrhage' position. Failure to heal files severe cases. Is the suicide attempt of Gregor and Georg matched with it? It doesn't involve simply suicide; it explodes multiple screw loss crises. It leaves many invisible scapegoats behind. When a high-ranking official pressures an employee to complete a task on time, it reminds us of the Mary Anne Walkley issue.

If a man is fearless of being fired; he can do good work. It depends on the company's atmosphere, the owner, society, and the family. With staying cool, no one losses a mental screw. A soft, supportive, and kind environment is the best remedy for them. We often hear that a man had committed suicide. But we rarely trace to know the reason. We become skeptical; that is, blame. Blame is more dangerous than AK 47. Several characters in Kafkaesque are blamed and scapegoated like Gregor, Georg, and Joseph.

Sometimes suicide follows sheep tendency. Suppose, society is in suicidal tendencies; it develops a suicide atmosphere. Presume A, B, C, and D did suicide for various reasons. E and the rest drain in the same river. For a moment it needs reason and other times reason-less. The philosophical dam needs to wall itself from the Camusian flow. That is an emergence in Fearism terminology.

*Joseph Garcin, *Inez Serrano, and *Estelle Rigault committed a crime and were sent to hell. Any action must have been caused. Sisyphus was chastised by God. To take such chastise, god had a source. If not take that deed; tomorrow, no one respects them. It was the motive to take action. Divinity believed that it makes Sisyphus(es) fear and takes sheep's tendency. Again, Sisyphus had a root of cunning which was a drought in Corinth and the temptation of the world. It caused deception between Thanatos and Hades.

A man looks for values in life. In weakness and failure, he feels sad. The futility of life is not the cause of self-trigger bullets. Samsa and Bendemann are the best examples. If a boss is a sadist, he always terrorizes. He loses endurance and mental state. Failure provokes self-hammer. If a man has no fear of being terminated, the personal and domestic burden, financial problems, relationship break up, chronic pain, illness, conflict, disaster, violence, abuse, loss, and a sense of isolation, he can do the best performance. In a compassionate environment, a crisis ends, and success and happiness come.

A lot of cases come when there is a mental calamity. People have private, communal, and national fears. Mostly negative fear leads to suicide, communal leads to struggle, and national leads to revolution. The metamorphosis of the Camusian version changes their suicidal state.

PHILOSOPHICAL GATE WAY

The philosophical problem is a 'Jingle Bell' question. A person wants to come out from his barriers and populace shell. Garcin tried to exit from hell. He rang a bell. No one came to open the door for him. The chain of the populace is Sisyphus(es). Every man tries to blow through Sisyphus, but it is a concrete wall. He plays multiple roles. One man shoves a stone, the empirical man gazes downward to the earth and the rational man stares at the sky. That way, nobody makes him free; he is decorated in a matter and pasted on the wall. He has to break laces and find out who bounds him in the underworld. Who made him Sisyphus?

God bound Sisyphus, but the average man is bound by self. Joseph Garcin, Inez, and Estelle are examples.

Failing forces one to end the life; it is absurdist reckoning. Sisyphus crisis is a Camusian crisis. Homer did not swim in that ocean. Kafka's torture, murder, and suicide case comes under a super scapegoat structure. Sisyphus swims in any direction. It doesn't have Google Maps.

Among multiple treks, absurd is a terminal. Camusian horizon terminates here. Color of the rainbow changes. At this critical moment, suppose this idea drops for a while. It embodied the bright world. Any failure doesn't force us to end our life; it boosts us to climb the peak.

Camus believes falling stone is a happy moment because no need to push up. It is possible in myth but in practical life, it is absurd. In philosophical terms, to not believe in any philosophy is a philosophy.

To be a liberal man and enjoy freedom, he must be free from stones. A stone metamorphoses a man into Sisyphus. The shadowed part of him is the terror of rock. At mistake, a satanic rock can dust him. When Satan is dancing in the head everything goes dim, only comes fear. It comes from lousy faith (Sartre), superstructure (Karl Marx), cultural hegemony (Gramsci), and super fear structure (Subba). Avoidance is impossible because we are on its target. In medieval Europe size of the stone was Typhonic. A light of liberalization was its boon.

Opinions differ as to the reasons why he became the futile laborer of the underworld [20]. Camus has left a space for multidisciplinary studies. Man is condemned to be free and man is condemned to be enslaved. Why did slave Sisyphus, not revolt? Why was he like an honest bull pulling a cart? Mythically, it was his fate, practically it was his boulder. One punishment is enough to ruin a life what happens if more punishments are added? His dread stopped him from revolting. Was terror only to him? Thanatos and Hades had too. It was fear vs fear wrestling. Their fear was if not punished, a worse situation will appear.

Homer writes,

> And on his tip-toes racking all his height.
> To wrest up to a mountain-top his freight;

Camus rewrites, "The gods had condemned Sisyphus to ceaselessly rolling a rock to the top of the mountain, whence the stone would fall back of its weight" [21].

Why had gods condemned Sisyphus? It is a metaphosphoric and realistic question forever. Philosophers have given various theories. Fearism forwards its standpoint. Not merely condemned Sisyphus, he had been punished ceaselessly rolling a rock to the top of the mountain. The nature of punishment varies, in one sense, a stone is nominal, and futile labour is the biggest punishment according to Camus, for "They had thought with some reason that there is no more dreadful punishment than futile and hopeless labour" [22].

Then Sisyphus watches the stone rush down in a few moments towards that lower world whence he will have to push it up again toward the summit [23].

The stone rushes down and terrors him. When the stone rushes down, it represents the despicable condition. Rolling down position is down rush'd the deadly quarry.

Happiness and the absurd are two sons of the same earth. They are inseparable. It would be a mistake to say that happiness necessarily springs from an absurd discovery. It happens as well that the feelings of the absurd spring from happiness [24].

I do not agree with Camus. Happiness and fear are two sons of the same earth and the sky is more logical. When football players won the world cup, they felt happy. Not only they felt, the nation felt proud. How did they achieve pride? Students, players, businessmen, or any man fear failure, defeat, loss, and unsuccess. It motivates, forces, and conducts them as *Bhageeratha. After hard work, they succeed and feel happy.

There is no sun without shadow, and it is essential to know the night [25].

Sun represents bright and the shadow represents dark. Intriguingly it peeps in daily life. But, fear was always in the dark, and philosophers could not see it. Yin is cold, empty, dark, and passive and Yang is active and bright in Yin Yang philosophy. For example, Mug is Yang and Yin is tea. Without emptiness in Mug, we cannot fill tea [26]. The 21st-century Fearists came and saw the light of fear (Yin) because Yang was already there. They are showing a beautiful universe. Jacques Derrida used binary opposition and gap idea from Yin Yang.

One must imagine Sisyphus happy [27].

How do we imagine somebody happy in Naraka? Were Joseph Garcin, Inez Serrano, and Estelle Rigault happy? Can a man be delighted in a body straining to raise the huge stone? His point is falling with stone time. In the mouth of the monster, no one can be cheerful. Between pushing and falling the rock, where is a happy moment? If the falling moment is the happiest then being jobless would be a golden time. In contrast, jobless always have worry, tension, restlessness, and fear.

Sisyphus's life was fearful. That's why he escapes all the time. His levity, scorn, hatred of god, passion, and escape made him fear Sisyphus. It is the clear version of Socrates that an unjust man's life is like the life of an unhealthy person. An unhealthy person is never blissful. Fraud, cheater, liar, rascal, and immoral man is unjust and sick. His days are in Gyges Ring and the Panopticons. Hiding, escaping, and running is his time. Then, how can he be pleased? In our connection, there are many high-alert Homerian Sisyphuses. During, eating, and sleeping, they have a nightmare of the Panopticons.

Camus has highlighted the fate of man in many places. I have noted some of them which is a link to my objective;

a. In this unintelligible and limited universe, man's fate henceforth assumes its meaning [28].

b. A fate is not a punishment [29].

c. Our fate stands before us and we provoke him [30].

d. At each of those moments when he leaves the heights and gradually sinks toward the lairs of gods, he is superior to his fate [31].

e. There is no fate that cannot be surmounted by scorn [32].

f. Thus, Oedipus at the outset obeys fate without knowing it [33].

g. It makes of fate a human matter, which must be settled among men [34].

h. His fate belongs to him [35].

i. If there is a personal fate, there is no higher destiny, or at least there is but one which he concludes is inevitable and despicable [36].

j. At that subtle moment when man glances backward over his life, Sisyphus returning toward his rock, in that slight pivoting he contemplates that series of unrelated actions which becomes his fate, created by him, combined under his memory's eye, and soon sealed by his death [37].

Dr. Isaac Madok writes, Kant argues, "Human reason has this peculiar fate that in one species of its knowledge it is burdened by questions which, as prescribed by the very nature of reason itself, it is not able to ignore, but which, as transcending all its powers, it is also not able to answer" [38].

Sisyphus and rock are the fate of believers. They are metaphoric scapegoats. Before the medieval era, it was applied by the ruling class and priests. According to Camus, Sisyphus represents us who works every day in our life at the same tasks. Fate represents the employee of today. It was criticized by Sartre. In this context, a. Fate precedes essence (Aristotle). b. Existence precedes fate (Sartre).

For the Greeks, values pre-existed all actions, of which they definitely set the limits. Modern philosophy places its values at the end of action [39].

Regarding it, what fate of Sisyphus (Camus) has, was explained long ago. After reading him, I contemplated a mad and insane man. Why they don't look at fate (essence)? It stroked my mind and synthesized that the c. existence of fear precedes fate (Subba).

Nobody looks at Sisyphus from multiple folds, only overview as prisoners (Allegory of Cave). He was a fidelities prisoner of hell. His life was an absurdity; it is Camus's eye. The audience has a magnifying glass to speculate on Sisyphus. Camus wanted to show the absurd part. Sartre wanted to show hell. The stone and its grinding teeth are not noticed. Someone reached near the mouth of the Hydra and said, "I am standing here because life is absurd." Doesn't it seem ridiculous? He attempted to prove birth of a man is futile. Its disappearance part is more mysterious. The sky, environment, and nature are out of focus.

God, stone, Sisyphus Mountain, sun, cloud, environment, Tartarus, curse, punishment, and emotions have an active role. It is a union of consciousness (man) and matter (stone). The Law of Motion can be applied. In what ratio pushes up the boulder and digital ratio it falls down. On one side, Sisyphus hardly shoves upward, and on another side, the obstacle pulls downward. Drive-up a rock doesn't make any sense to him, but a U-turn is dangerous to him. In life, we always push a stone and handle it with care because, at any moment, it grinds and makes us dust. Up and down is absurd; and, what then is the stone and fear of a man? The wonderful answer is miraculously lost.

Society is under a fear hierarchy. It is made by fear manv; it made a faithful community. The government runs on its basis. Why did Thanatos and Hades be so cruel to Sisyphus? Why do governments punish anyone? Why did Hermann Kafka close the door for his nine year old son Franz Kafka? The sentence of Sisyphus, Garcin, Inez, and Estelle are dissimilar. Fear of God and criminal fear are different (Using the idea of James Stuart Mill; Mill argues, that the pleasure of poems and Ice cream is the contrast).

We want to keep law and order. Its purpose is to keep peace and bliss. Fear is the ruler of heaven, earth, and the underworld. It judges a person, society, and state. Punishment of Sisyphus makes it free to a mass people. It is a spinning stone; the accused has to rotate it till the end of his sentence. Everyone is bound by the law and the law is bound by fear.

We have three Sisyphuses: 1. Cunning Sisyphus (Homer) 2. Proletariat Sisyphus (Camus) 3. Fear Sisyphus (Subba). Another way we can see the thesis, antithesis, and synthesis of Sisyphus. The common among the three is a boulder. It is like Deconstruction (Derrida), Leela Writing (Rai I.B. & Dharabasi), and Fearmorphosis (Subba).

Nicola Tenerelli opines, "The hidden purpose of the mighty volume is to show the contemporary subject how to understand its complexity in order to become a master of himself: this result can only be achieved by seeking the anfang of human action, understanding what is the fulcrum that moves human life. The philosopher manages to Trans philosophism (sic!) By deconstructing history, and creating a genealogy of humanity: he will thus discover that the principle from which historical existence moves is fear; the author can therefore state, paraphrasing Existentialism is a humanism" [40].

The critic from India, Kabir Basnet, has attempted to look at Vijay Malla's 'The Story of Stone' one-act play from a fearism point of view. He writes, "At present fearism seems to be advancing as a popular theory. This ideology carries the idea that every human's activity is driven by fear" [41].

Deepak Subedi, applied Fearism in B. P. Koirala's story; "Koirala, who accepts himself as a socialist, exposes fear inherited in human beings as the open and naked version in his stories. Under the theory of "Philosophy of Fearism," the basic idea of human life is "fear" and that "fear" leads the us" [42].

The final cause of a man is happiness, Aristotle said. I asked a question in an article what was the final cause of lockdown and quarantine during Covid-19? It was apprehension. Simply, we can see, Sisyphus disobeyed the gods and rolled a big rock. It is the same as the character of *No Exit*. Why did Sisyphus not break the order? Disobey caused harder punishment. Causes of series were the other cause of curses. The causes of the curse rounded around the cause. It links with subsistence, protection, and death. A drought of Ephyra was the base of the fable. It birthed many causes and effects. 1. Subject (Sisyphus) 2. Object (God) 3. Punishment (action) was involved. God's terror is veiled.

HELL IS NO OTHER PEOPLE

I am distinguishing and imagining *No Exit* of Sartre into two parts. He has shown it in one part. It is like a chapter of the book. Without knowing chapter one, we cannot decide the consequences of chapter two. In chapter one, they have Karma. Karm[a] is a major factor: go to hell or heaven. In practice, whether somebody is sent to jail or remains in an open space is decided by Karma. In jail, we never expect a heavenly life. The character of Sartre is expectant. When he was nine months in Padoux, maybe he expected it. He was captured by German Army in 1940 as a prisoner of war. This expectation is hell itself.

Part One

INEZ: What have you done? I mean, why have they sent you here?

GARCIN: Let that be. It's only a side-issue. I'm here because I treated my wife abominably. That's all. For five years. Naturally, she's suffering still. There she is: the moment I mention her, I see her. It's Gomez who interests me, and it's she I see. Where's Gomez got to? For five years. There! They've given her back my things; she's sitting by the window, with my coat on her knees. The coat with the twelve bullet-holes. The blood's like rust; a brown ring round each hole. It's quite a museum-piece, that coat; scarred with history. And I used to wear it, fancy! . . . Now, can't you shed a tear, my love! Surely you'll squeeze one out—at last? No? You can't manage it? . . . Night after night I came home blind drunk, stinking of wine and women. She'd sat up for me, of course. But she never cried, never uttered a word of reproach. Only her eyes spoke. Big, tragic eyes. I don't regret anything. I must pay the price, but I shan't whine. . . . It's snowing in the street. Won't you cry, confound you? That woman was a born martyr, you know; a victim by vocation.

ESTELLE: There was a balcony overlooking the lake. I brought a big stone. He could see what I was up to and he kept on shouting: "Estelle, for God's sake, don't!" I hated him then. He saw it all. He was leaning over the balcony and he saw the rings spreading on the water.

INEZ: No. There was that affair with Florence. A dead men's tale. With three corpses to it. He to start with; then she and I. So there's no one left, I've nothing to worry about; it was a clean sweep. Only that room. I see it now and then. Empty, with the doors locked. . . . No, they've just un-locked them. "To Let." It's to let; there's a notice on the door. That's—too ridiculous.

GARCIN: So much the better. So much the better for you. I suppose all this strikes you as very vague. Well, here's some-thing you can get your teeth into. I brought a half-caste girl to stay in our house. My wife slept upstairs; she must have heard—everything. She was an early riser and, as I and the girl stayed in bed late, she served us our morning coffee.

ESTELLE: What else should I tell? I've nothing to hide. I lost my parents when I was a kid, and I had my young brother to bring up. We were terribly poor and when an old friend of my people asked me to marry him I said yes. He was very well off, and quite nice. My brother was a very delicate child and needed all sorts of attention, so really that was the right thing for me to do, don't you agree? My husband was old enough to be my father, but for six years we had a happy married life. Then two years ago I met the man I was fated to love. We knew it the moment we set eyes on each other. He asked me to run away with him, and I refused. Then I got pneumonia and it finished me. That's the whole story. No doubt, by certain standards, I did wrong to sacrifice my youth to a man nearly three times my age. [To GARCIN] Do you think that could be called a sin?

GARCIN: Wait a bit! I ran a pacifist newspaper. Then war broke out. What was I to do? Everyone was watching me, wondering: "Will he dare?" Well, I dared. I folded my arms and they shot me. Had I done anything wrong?

INEZ: I'll tell you later. When I say I'm cruel, I mean I can't get on without making people suffer. Like a live coal. A live coal in others' hearts. When I'm alone I flicker out. For six months I flamed away in her heart, till there was nothing but a cinder. One night she got up and turned on the gas while I was asleep. Then she crept back into bed. So now you know.

GARCIN: This bronze. [Strokes it thoughtfully.] Yes, now's the moment; I'm looking at this thing on the mantelpiece, and I understand that I'm in hell. I tell you, everything's been thought out beforehand. They knew I'd stand at the fire-place stroking this thing of bronze, with all those eyes intent on me. Devouring me. [He swings round abruptly.] What? Only two of you? I thought there were more; many more. [Laughs.] So this is hell. I'd never have believed it. You re-member all we were told about the torture-chambers, the fire and brimstone, the "burning marl." Old wives' tales! There's no need for red-hot pokers.

INEZ: Yes, we are criminals—murderers—all three of us. We're in hell, my pets; they never make mistakes, and people aren't damned for nothing.

***

"Hell is other people" is a famous quote from Sartre. Is it right? I asked. Was Hell of Hitler, Saddam's made by other people? I don't think so. 90% of Hell is made by self. Only 10% is made by other people.

Hell of Sisyphus is not made by other people. The consequence of his cunning Karma is the source. First Sartre said existence precedes essence, now this is said by other people. He is inconsistent. If we deeply analyse it, we can find the answer. The answer is in the first question of Inez. Poor countries are living in Hell. Corrupted leaders cause hell and scapegoat people and nations. Student A does hard to study and gets a distinct mark. He finds a high-salary job. It is his heaven. Student B doesn't do labour, he always fails the exam. In the future, he doesn't find a good job. His life is hard, low income, and low respect. It is his hell. Criminals, gamblers, drinkers, lazy, cheaters, and liars make hell themselves.

We have many examples. So, Hell is no other people, Sisyphus, Garcia, Inez, Estelle, Saddam, Hitler, and many criminals, kidnappers, killers, and corrupters, went to hell. Were they by others? No. It was themselves. Hell is hell. If we step into a thorn, how can we expect flowers? Both Camus or Sartre misinterprets. Camus underestimates boulder and Sartre forgot to mention the origin of hell. The primary cause was their crime. Who does crime and expects heaven, it is absurd. He focused on secondary cause that directly opened the curtain and shows hell. Can we anticipate heaven from hell? Sartre awaited it.

There are two parts to drama; which we must emphasize first. The first clearly confessed they did the crime and murderers. The crime was done by themselves and scapegoated others. When other people decide their fate (life), then it is contradictory. Sartre's philosophy splits.

The prisoners are criminals and murderers. They are in hell because of Karma. The room of *No Exit* is hell. "Hell is other people" quote can be metamorphosized as Sisyphus and Leela.

Part Two

In the first part, we saw they are hell for themselves. Some of the examples I have given above.

GARCIN: Frightened! But how ridiculous! Of whom should they be frightened? Of their victims?

INEZ: They look frightened.

GARCIN: In the glass? [He looks around him.] How beastly of them! They've removed everything in the least resembling a glass. [Short silence.] Anyhow, I can assure you I'm not frightened. Not that I take my position lightly; I realize its gravity only too well. But I'm not afraid.

INEZ: That's just what I reproach you with. [GARCIN'S mouth twitches.] There you are! You talk about politeness, and you don't even try to control your face. Remember you're not alone; you've no right to inflict the sight of your fear on me.

GARCIN [getting up and going towards her]: How about you? Aren't you afraid?

INEZ: What would be the use? There was some point in being afraid before; while one still had hope.

ESTELLE [still laughing]: It's those sofas. They're so hideous. And just look how they've been arranged. It makes me think of New Year's Day—when I used to visit that boring old aunt of mine, Aunt Mary. Her house is full of horrors like that. . . . I suppose each of us has a sofa of his own. Is that one mine? [To the VALET] But you can't expect me to sit on that one. It would be too horrible for words. I'm in pale blue and it's vivid green.

GARCIN: Twelve bullets through my chest. [Estelle makes a horrified gesture.] Sorry! I fear I'm not good company among the dead.

ESTELLE: Please, please don't use that word. It's so—so crude. In terribly bad taste, really. It doesn't mean much, anyhow. Somehow I feel we've never been so much alive as now. If we've absolutely got to mention this—this state of things, I suggest we call ourselves—wait!— absentees. Have you been—been absent for long?

INEZ: Exactly. That's the question. Was that your real motive? No doubt you argued it out with yourself, you weighed the pros and cons, you found good reasons for what you did. But fear and hatred and all the dirty little instincts one keeps dark—they're motives too. So carry on, Mr. Garcin, and try to be honest with yourself—for once.

ESTELLE. Oh, I don't know. You scare me rather.

INEZ: There. . . . You know the way they catch larks—with a mirror? I'm your lark-mirror, my dear, and you can't escape me. . . . There isn't any pimple, not a trace of one. So what about it? Suppose the mirror started telling lies? Or suppose I covered my eyes—as he is doing—and refused to look at you, all that loveliness of yours would be wasted on the desert air. No, don't be afraid, I can't help looking at you. I shan't turn my eyes away. And I'll be nice to you, ever so nice. Only you must be nice to me, too. [A short silence.]

ESTELLE: What a quaint thing to ask! Considering you'll be under my eyes all the time, and I don't think I've much to fear from Inez, so far as you're concerned.

GARCIN: Then why should you have been so scared? He blew his brains out, didn't he? That's how his face got smashed.

INEZ: You know quite well. The man you were so scared of seeing when you came in.

GARCIN: Why were you afraid of him?

INEZ: Oh, I don't count? Is that what you think? But, my poor little fallen nestling, you've been shelty ring in my heart for ages, though you didn't realize it. Don't be afraid; I'll keep looking at you for ever and ever, without a flutter of my eyelids, and you'll live in my gaze like a mote in a sunbeam.

GARCIN: And you know what wickedness is, and shame, and fear. There were days when you peered into yourself, into the secret places of your heart, and what you saw there made you faint with horror. And then, next day, you didn't I know what to make of it, you couldn't interpret the horror you had glimpsed the day before. Yes, you know what evil costs. And when you say I'm a coward, you know from experience what that means. Is that so?

ESTELLE: Oh, what a nuisance you are! I'm giving you my mouth, my arms, my whole body— and everything could be so simple. . . . My trust! I haven't any to give, I'm afraid, and you're making me terribly embarrassed. You must have something pretty ghastly on your conscience to make such a fuss about my trusting you.

GARCIN [putting his hands on her shoulders]: Listen! Each man has an aim in life, a leading motive; that's so, isn't it? Well, I didn't give a damn for wealth, or for love. I aimed at being a real man. A tough, as they say. I staked everything on the same horse. . . . Can one possibly be a coward when one's deliberately courted danger at every turn? And can one judge a life by a single action?

INEZ: Wait! You'll see how simple it is. Childishly simple. Obviously there aren't any physical torments—you agree, don't you? And yet we're in hell. And no one else will come here. We'll stay in this room together, the three of us, for ever and ever. . . . In short, there's someone absent here, the official torturer.

GARCIN: Open the door! Open, blast you! I'll endure anything, your red-hot tongs and molten lead, your racks and prongs and garrotes— all your fiendish gadgets, everything that burns and flays and tears— I'll put up with any torture you impose. Anything, anything would be better than this agony of mind, this creeping pain that gnaws and fumbles and caresses one and never hurts quite enough. [He grips the door-knob and rattles it.] Now will you open? [The door flies open with a jerk, and he just avoids falling.] Ah! [A long silence.] Hell is—other people! [43].

***

Such kinds of many hells are all over the world. Either voluntary exile, hiding, or punishment by authority, or the enemy takes them to the semi and the full Tartarus.

In this play, Sartre used danger, coward, scare, fear, afraid, frightened, horror, terrible, hurt, and torture, in several dialogues. Mostly we don't notice them. These are feariers. If we see from Fearism point of view, we can say fearist play.

Dr. Bhawani Shankar Adhikari said in a conversation, "Dante's concept of hell is based on nine circles and ten ditches for the earthly sinners to sentence after physical death whereas seven major and other twenty-eight hells are stated in *The Garudamahapuram* of Vedvyas for the Earthly sinners to punish after physical death on Earth." Adhikari is a PhD. holder in the portrayal of Punishment and Fear in Vedavyasa's *The Garudamahapuranam* and Dante Alighieri's *Inferno*.

Abdullateef A. Sadiq reviews, "here goes Mr. Desh Subba again after his book *Philosophy of Fearism*, where he expounds (I have discussed that critically somewhere else) the basic arguments regarding the role, structure, and function of fear throughout the varieties of human experience. The task he set himself there was to bring to the foreground the structure and dynamics of fear throughout the world of human experience and speculations and as they find their practical purpose or utility in the material organization of the external/objective 'world.' He takes the pain to classify the broad categories of the human experience of fear in whatever aspects" [44].

Some thinkers, warriors, politicians, and scientists spend much of their life in the underworld. For example, the underworld of Karl Marx is England, Albert Einstein's underworld is the United States, Niccolò Machiavelli was in Florence, Aristotle Euboea, Napoleon Bonaparte Saint Helena, Adolf Hitler Fuhrerbunker, and Saddam Hussein, Camp Justice. Some were exiled, some were punished, some migrated, some took refuge and some escaped. Sartre's hell is Padoux. One of the very famous underworlds was Port Blair, Andaman, and Nicobar Islands. Freedom fighters of India were sentenced there. The United States is a superpower nation, its president hides in a bunker from time to time. Their superpower cannot penetrate fear, fear shoots their bullet, bomb, and missile, proof vehicles. They are fear presidents (Sisyphus).

***

End Notes

1. Subba (2021a).
2. Camus (1955), p. 90.
3. Johansen (2021).
4. Dharabasi (2017), pp. 26-27.
5. Ibid., p. 83.
6. Subba (2014), pp. 60, 203.
7. Subba (2021b), p. 46.
8. Ibid., p. 9.
9. Subba (2021b) classified "fear struggle" and "fear sapiens" and "fear heritage" (historically) and "fear as gravity" to look deeply at "Basic Laws of Fearological Materialism" (*contra*, Marxist doctrine); see e.g., pp. 138-40—all, conceptions underpinning his philosophy of fearmorphism and links with the Sisyphus myth (especially, the "stone" and "fear as gravity" are self-evident).
10. Subba (2021b), p. 404.
11. Derrida (1976).

12. Camus (1955), p. 90.
13. Ibid., p. 17.
14. Homer, pp. 639-40.
15. Camus, p. 89.
16. Ibid.
17. King (2019).
18. Camus (1955), p. 89.
19. Ibid., p. 15.
20. Ibid., p. 88.
21. Ibid.
22. Ibid.
23. Ibid., p. 89.
24. Ibid., p. 90.
25. Ibid., p. 91.
26. https://www.youtube.com/watch?v=7W3PfJjzanQ
27. Camus (1955), p. 91.
28. Ibid., p. 16.
29. Ibid., p. 55.
30. Ibid., p. 67.
31. Ibid., p. 89.
32. Ibid., p. 90.
33. Ibid., p. 90.
34. Ibid., p. 91.
35. Ibid.
36. Ibid.
37. Ibid.
38. Ibid., p. 136.
39. https://fearlessnessmovement.ning.com/blog/critique-of-philosophy-of-fearism=show?commentId=6662424%3AComment%3A29538&xg_source=msg_com_blogpost
40. https://fearlessnessmovement.ning.com/blog/Trans-Philosophism-book-review
41. https://sahityapost.com/gair-aakhyan/gair-aakhyan-samaalochna/63278/?fbclid=IwAR0vCvhBQnFp6j3MEgVTr6k4ht-gYg-Qk0tYrC5fk_rWgTp9roQ9pM0I-pg
42. https://fearlessnessmovement.ning.com/blog/philosophy-of-fearism-in-bp-koirala-s-stories-a-critical-approach
43. file:///Users/limbunisham/Downloads/Jean-Paul_Sartre.pdf
44. https://taffds.org/11605-https://taffds.org/11605-2/?fbclid=IwAR3VwDbbjNWLA_dnGNZXxsBaB9xOvXkzXtm7ZJqqeCmxWRCLBnOiak9AJeY

*Gregor Samsa is the main character of *The Metamorphosis* book of Franz Kafka. It is detailed explanation is in part five.

*Ganges's is in part four legend of Bhageeratha

*Bhageeratha was a king in north India. He did hard penance to bring the Ganges from the sky to Earth. The Ganges is a symbol of water. Hard penance is also known as hard work or Bhageeratha effort. Its myth comes in part four.

*Antonio is a character in the play *The Merchant of Venice* by Shakespeare.

*Georg is a character in *The Judgment*

*Joseph K. is a character in *The Trial*

*Joseph Garcin, Inez Serrano, and Estelle Rigault are characters in the *No Exit* play.

PART TWO

MORALITY

THE ALLEGORY OF PANOPTICON

We have many fables about Panopticons; ethics, epics, and grand narrations. The Allegory of Panopticon is a collective ambassador of them.

A human is a Panopticon. The Panopticon is by the man, to the man, and for the man. It is a symbolic name; being watched by someone.

Civilization, and culture tried to develop a just human. According to time, various forms of Panopticons changed. It was a fearological device to bind people in forms of discipline.

They didn't yet invent CCTV in the early days of civilization. They brought the concept of imaginary eyes of God, evil, nature, and ghost. Whatever names were given, they were the watching eyes.

Developed forms of eyes were fate, heaven, hell, demon, and God. At present, the latest technology is chips, long-distance binoculars, and satellites. Mobile phone chips are a major issue of the Panopticons. Recently, US and China have had a controversy over the Balloon Panopticon.

Panopticon can be any device. Before it was merely limited to people, now, it applies from one country to another country, one space to another space. Many agencies, institutions, and organizations are working on eyes. In the past, the purpose of its institutionalization was to control immoral folks into morals. At present, it is used to spy on individuals, societies, and nations. Its telos are constant. To simplify, telos came to physical Panopticons. We have ideological and physical Panopticons.

a. Spiritual Panopticon

Eye Motif or Evil Eye

Eda Uzumlar writes in *Washington Post*, the *evil eye* symbol has been found through thousands of years of history across cultures, including in Latin America and some parts of Asia. The symbol, most often depicted as four concentric circles in the shape of an eye, is used to ward off variations of evil intentions.

In much of the Middle East and North Africa, the symbol wards off "nazar" — a curse motivated by the envy of others that can bring about bad things in your life. This fear of envy can keep you from being boastful or too sure; but it can also keep you from celebrating your accomplishments or pursuing success in the first place. It even made me hesitant to make this comic — the evil eye is always watching [1].

The first Panopticon concept was born in some allegories in Latin America and some parts of Asia. Its history goes thousands of years across cultures. The purpose was to ward off variations of evil intentions like fear of envy. It controls being boastful and celebrates success. We think the eye is always watching our activities; we follow morality because the invisible eye is scanning us. So, we have to perform a righteous role in family, society, and nation. When we carry out as good citizens, we get success and happiness.

In early times, this idea was developed to build a moral and virtuous society. It is still applicable. When we tell ethical stories to a child, we say, "Don't go out in the evening because the ghost is watching you." With fright of ghost, children stop doing naughty activities supposedly. It is good for children, parents, and society. Thus, such ethical studies include in the syllabus to give them morality. At present, social media is making the spiritual Panopticon more popular.

b. Ideological Panopticon

Many kinds of physical and theoretical Panopticons are used at present. We frequently see and listen to 'voice' on sound system in bus, train, and door "Keep an eye on your belongings" and "Theft: liable to imprisonment." Sometimes "Beware of Pickpockets." In theory, basically, three ideas can be applied.

Jeremy Bentham Stage

Jeremy Bentham was a social theorist. He uses it originally for prisoners. According to him, a prisoner never knew; he was being watched. A circular prison with a single guard tower in the middle was the original blueprint for the structure. The guard tower, manned by a single sniper, was hypothesized to be all it would take to manipulate the prisoners to be well-behaved. Though there are no prisons that fit Bentham's Panopticon directly, around thirty prisons have cited architectural influence. The design of the Panopticon fostered behavior modification based on the possibility of an omniscient guard. While historically and religiously, this behavior modification is based on omniscience and has been seen before, with the Egyptian all-seeing eye and several monotheistic texts referring to an omniscient deity, 20th, and 21st-century literature has seen an increase in omniscient people and things. In the modern age, the Panopticon has become an allegory for a loss of privacy, particularly with modern conveniences like the internet and CCTV [2].

Bentham's idea was disciplinary. He brought it to life in the form of a central observation tower placed within a circle of prison cells. From the tower, a watchman can observe each cell and inmate but the inmates can't see him. Inmates think they are being watched by a guard. When someone is looking, we hesitate, are nervous, shy, inferior, and awful. For a person to live in such ordered societies they have to follow discipline, rule, law, culture, religion, morality, and system. Breach of it can be costly, as they can face lots of hells. It is the reason, one must be moral. Communities are gentler because of moral citizens.

Michel Foucault Stage

Michel Foucault writes, the Panopticon is a privileged place for experiments on humans, and for analyzing with complete certainty the transformations that may be obtained from them.

The Panopticon may even provide an apparatus for supervising its own mechanisms. In this central tower, the director may spy on all the employees that he has under his orders: nurses, doctors, foremen, teachers, and warders; he will be able to judge them continuously; even alter their behavior, impose upon them the methods he thinks best; and it will even be possible to observe the director himself. An inspector arriving unexpectedly at the center of the Panopticon will be able to judge at a glance, without anything being concealed from him, how the entire establishment is functioning.

And, in any case, enclosed as he is in the middle of this architectural mechanism, is not the director's own fate entirely bound up with it? The incompetent physician who has allowed contagion to spread, the incompetent prison governor or workshop manager will be the first victims of an epidemic or a revolt. "By every tie I could devise," said the master of the Panopticon, "my own fate had been bound up by me with theirs" (Bentham, 177). The Panopticon functions as a kind of laboratory of power. Thanks to its mechanisms of observation, it gains in efficiency and in the ability to penetrate into men's behavior; knowledge follows the advances of power, discovering new objects of knowledge over all the surfaces on which power is exercised [3].

Foucault highlighted his idea in Bentham's idea, "From the central tower, the inspector spy all." He extended inmates to many spheres of society and how it monitors their behavior, imposing upon them the methods he thinks best. He said the Panopticon functions as a kind of laboratory of power, his focus is on power.

My argument is, nurses, doctors, foremen, teachers, warders, politicians, religious, merchants, and the rest, are fearful that someone is watching them. A guard himself is not out of the viewing eye. Nowadays, a new idea is applied. On the top of his head, one camera is fixed. That camera surveillance system includes the guard. He views all the cameras from the guard room but on top of his head it looks at him from somewhere. He is being watched by the spiritual and physical Panopticons.

This system maintains social, law, and order. Law and order is a weapon and a Panopticon is an education in another sense. Why do we take education? Why do we have a hospital? In absence of education, the future may be dark and with the unavailability of hospitals, we may die for a nominal reason. Every individual has, more or less, some intimidated by a particular Panopticon.

In the class, teachers and administrates may choose a monitor to view students. They are a Panopticon of the class. The Head of the state is the monitor of the nation, as they judged and monitor the people. In conclusion, fear of being watched by guards, all inmates, more or less, keep good behavior, moral, honesty, loyal, punctuality, and hard work. Foucault's idea of the Panopticon is limited to society.

Desh Subba Stage

As a fearist, I apply Panopticon somewhat distinct from Bentham and Foucault. The Panopticon idea can be used for Sisyphus.

Any Sisyphus (es) rolls a stone (Part One) because they think, they have been watched by someone. Owning of that they perform the regular task and be polite, honest, moral, and humble. Being scanned by someone is an external part. It has an internal part too. The external part can be ignored but the internal is impossible. A man is always between internal and external Panopticons.

Government, society, school, business, hospital, and God are being viewed. The myth of Sisyphus is not exceptional. His

Panopticon is kept somewhere. We are inmates in one particular sense. The superstructure of Karl Marx and the Super Panopticon Structure are different. Super Panopticon Structure (SPS) is that no one easily knows it. For Bentham and Foucault it was used as the normal Panopticon.

I use it one step in advance, which is SPS. One can say the average Panopticon and the next can say special Panopticon. The driver, pilot, and captain have an internal Panopticon. Rule, law, and punishment are the Panopticon towers. It controls them. It is useful to use in Fearism, I'll explain.

Panopticon views immorality, misconduct, and misbehaving. But thieves, cheaters, rascals, killers, kidnappers, murderers, corruptors, blackmailers, and treason want to disappear from its eye. They use bribery to persuade the concerned person. They have the horror of being caught by someone. If they have a Gyges Ring, no one can see them. It has the opposite relation to Panopticon. At present, plastic surgery, mask, cap, glass, and dress are used to distinguish their original face and body. Only Panopticon is not enough to view the insight of travellers. So, at immigration examine external and internal body parts including shoe soles. The government tries to detect their criminal face. They invented many applications to view them. Particularly this scene can be seen in visa applications and immigration. The officer checks eyes, faces, and takes photos. They are concerned that some criminals may enter the country. Day by day various forms of Gyges Rings and Panopticon are co-developing in the world.

For example, somebody does not receive a phone call and always changes numbers. Some change home addresses and shift to an unknown place. On social media, they use a fake ID. These activities are forms of disappearance Ring.

CIA, MI6, KGB, and RAW are the intelligence and Panopticons of the state. Even terrorists, killers, robbers, and criminals play the role of Panopticon because we have been under surveillance by them.

It is the reason, the presidents, prime ministers, and businessmen use bulletproof cars. Sometimes the role of Gyges Ring and sometimes Panopticon is like a thief *and* police. So, I argue for universal, international, and national SPS. Social Panopticon makes a righteous society, but an international one makes a just global village. Metaphysical Panopticon keeps the universe in order. My concept goes to the world and universe; they are also under surveillance. The Panopticon has level 1. The guard looks at Inmate 2. Guard surveillance by somewhere and 3. Somewhere monitor by unknown cameras.

c. Physical Panopticon

Media Panopticon

Media Panopticon is widely spread in the present world. It looks everywhere and at everybody. Every man has a private and secret life. They hide themselves and their property. Thus, it is a hiding time. In another way, they want to expose everything in society.

The media eye is persistent and sharp. Several exposing schemes are emerging every day. Any case, accident, or event can be live and viral within minutes. We are hungry to see and listen to such news. Which channel exposes more privacy of politicians, businessmen, and celebrities, then that media is quickly popularised. Their TRP (Television Rating Point) rises up.

In the competition, media, journals, and photographers always hunt through private and public affairs, with no boundaries. Private, government, police, army, and agencies through media are spying everywhere. These try to control corruption, crime, terrorism, and misconduct and clean the nation. Those with cameras everywhere are powerful. Those countries are developed, which camera has more power, those countries are poor, which camera has less power. Media is a Panopticon in another term. Most countries have given the media Panopticon the fourth organ of the nation.

Mostly we can see businessmen, leaders, and celebrities who want to use the Gyges Ring. They want to be invisible from the media eye. Those who have illegal money, criminal cases, and corruption, are more horrified. They want to hide as much as possible. If Gyges Ring is on auction, they will bid the highest tender. They deposit illegal money to international banks. We read and see exposes news of their secret papers.

Wikipedia writes, The Pandora Papers are 11.9 million leaked documents with 2.9 terabytes of data that the International Consortium of Investigative Journalists (ICIJ) published beginning on 3 October 2021. The leak exposed the secret offshore accounts of 35 world leaders, including current and former presidents, prime ministers, and heads of state as well as more than 100 billionaires, celebrities, and business leaders. The news organizations of the ICIJ described the document leak as their most expansive exposé of financial secrecy yet, containing documents, images, emails, and spreadsheets from 14 financial service companies, in nations including Panama, Switzerland, and the United Arab Emirates, surpassing their previous release of the Panama Papers in 2016, which had 11.5 million confidential documents (2.6 terabytes). At the time of the release of the papers, the ICIJ said it is not identifying its source for the documents [4].

Paparazzi are another of the dangerous Panopticon for celebrities. The car accident of Lady Diana was caused by it according to BBC. Paparazzi are always behind the players, politicians, actors, actresses, and rich people. These high-profile publics are afraid of it. Banks and financial companies hire agencies for Panopticon work. Some customers take a loan from the bank and escape. Those fugitives are watched by the agency and submit reports.

Physical instruments may be different than Bentham and Foucault but the work is almost similar. Lots of media Panopticons are projected nowadays. Its role is for a healthy society. Sometimes, the media deals with illegal activities. Another Panopticon must need to watch them as CCTV surveillances a guard by the head camera.

d. Representative Panopticon

God and devil are sitting in the inspection house. This is the feeling of inmates, for example. In their eye, we are inmate Sisyphuses.

We sense God will punish us. God is always watching our activities. It can be used in morality, ethics, discipline, and sincerity. It builds the best society, apparently. We think people are in self-control, discipline, and morals. But no, they are controlled by unknown Panopticons. The watchman is behind goodness.

We can see everywhere CCTV, posters of two eyes. These are popular in Mahal, on bus, train, and public areas. Being watched by the Panopticon people, people tend to control themselves. Humans have long had fright of God's Panopticon. We can believe that God fears us. His agitation is, corrupting his kingdom. God, devil, spirit, and ghost have representative Panopticons. In some cases, they don't involve, their representatives do the Panopticons' duty like the priest. The form of the representative may be anything like a dummy scarecrow, but their task is to watch someone and prevent them from doing sin.

e. Hidden Panopticon

Plato had fear of corrupting his Kallipolis. He proposed three waves of revolution to turn Athens into an ideal state; A. Equal rights to women B. Communism of private property C. Rule of the philosopher king [5].

The lens is a Panopticon. If we look through Fearism lens, we can see everywhere, such Panopticons.

Plato gave the idea of precautions against abuse of power and instability of government. In this alarm, he has given sources of corruption: a. mind, b. family and private property, c. blood [6].

The question: Is an idea (and/or philosophy) a Panopticon? Yes, the philosopher is a watchman and theory is his Panopticon. He too takes part in their surveillances from their ideas.

People are inmates. In an autocracy, the dictator has more Panopticon vision; people are horrified that their ruler is watching them but the dictator is in more terror than the people. A democratic country also has this vision but less fear of rulers and *vice versa*.

A religious, moral, philosopher, politician, scientist, doctor, socialist, economist, astronomer, and astrologer's (Oracle of Delphi and Nostradamus) *eye* is a kind of Panopticon. They use predictive and astronomic cameras like weather report forecasts.

Many countries have shadow governments. We can see photos of dogs, animals, and danger. These are Panopticons of see, attack, accident, and hurt-risk perceptions. We have legal, health, security— and we have preservation, warnings, protection, damage, natural or otherwise, and we have a future—all with more hidden cameras. It cannot be viewed by the naked eye but can be sensed.

End Notes

1. https://www.washingtonpost.com/lifestyle/2022/07/10/evil-eye-isnt-just-trend-heres-what-it-means-me/
2. (https://the-artifice.com/panopticons-in-literature/?fbclid=IwAR3CzhnF8 ffY_CigIgHiFMBDIKtmn5nD0Mw1byrkf3dGIREOQCLfiwE0Hd4)
3. https://genius.com/Michel-foucault-discipline-and-punish-panopticon-excerpt-annotated?fbclid=IwAR0ViP1Amu7YawpM78b93zxqoHAOSl8Y8 KFDjokl0pl3GQfYsFfarHK917A
4. https://en.wikipedia.org/wiki/Pandora_Papers
5. https://www.youtube.com/watch?v=8dsRn95Lzp8&t=1682s
6. Ibid.

PART THREE

SCAPEGOAT

THE FABLE OF SCAPEGOAT

Dylan Ngan writes, Interpreting, and coping with the world, but reflecting upon our-self, psychology, and sense of meaning, how we come to live our lives [1].

The epical story of Troy is the scapegoat story of Helen. Likewise, the epics of Ramayana and Mahabharata are the scapegoat fable of Sita and Draupadi. The myth revolves around them.

To blockbuster, the story, millions of people were scapegoated in the fable. Sati system is the flopped story of it. Sati had to sit in the pyre of the deceased husband. Sita satied (I use the verb form of Sati) to the morality of Ram, Draupadi was staked in the gambling. They became victims and scapegoats in the name of love, truth, and morality.

Victimization is a scapegoat formation, in other words. Most religions, myths, beliefs, and epics are stories of scapegoats. We can see many scapegoats in politics, religion, morality, ethics, and culture. Typically the powerless is scapegoated.

Powerful fathers scapegoated their sons (Gregor, Georg, and Joseph K.). It can be seen in Kafkaesque writings. In the classes, communities, races, genders, fathers, and countries powerful enough, there is always the scapegoated of the powerless.

The master class, the priest, rich never are scapegoated. Small countries like Nepal, Taiwan, Bhutan, and Maldives always become scapegoats of superpower and great power countries.

In the conflict between the USA and China, Taiwan is scapegoated. Similarly, the battling between India and China; Nepal is scapegoated. Gregor was scapegoated in the conflict between the lodgers and the Samsa family. The war between Æsopus and Zeus Sisyphus was scapegoated. We never see small nations scapegoating the USA, China, and Russia.

Some years ago, there was a brutal civil war in Nepal. In war, the most scapegoated are the many civilians.

The myth is always recorded in the names of heroes and heroines. Scapegoats are discriminated, marginalized, and dominated in history.

Bali ko [ka] Boko (Bakara) is a commonly used scapegoat proverb in Nepal and India. Bali means sacrifice and Bakara means a goat. Pashu Bali is a synonym for it. Pashu means animal and Bali means sacrifice. We write Bali ko (ka) Boko (Bakara) (बलिका बकरा). The goat represents all kinds of sacrificial animals.

Mostly male animals are sacrificed. In case a female is sacrificed, it is also called Baliko Boko. Its full meaning is; to sacrifice a goat to God. Different sects of the Hindu religion sacrifice animals.

There are some communities that worship nature. People promise to God, and supposedly God makes them successful (for exam, business, job, desire, happiness, health, recovery of the patient, and recovery of damage, etc.). It is the devotee's belief. They promise, "I will offer you sweet, Coconut, and animal."

If somebody is looking for land, property, or business, at that time they promise to God and say, "God, make me successful, and I will offer an animal." They also pray, "God! Save me and my family."

Sometimes free walking and sitting bulls can be seen in the middle of a road in Kathmandu and some cities in India. Those are offered to Lord Shiva. They are free. In the West, they say, "Almighty God, grace me, save me, success me, bless me, forgiveness…".

The scapegoat doesn't have a single myth. Sisyphus has a single myth. One myth goes to scapegoat too. In several places, written in the Bible: it says, 'remove from sin.' What does sin mean? It is unclear.

Sinner gets punishment as Sisyphus, Joseph Garcin, Inez Serrano, and Estelle Rigault for their crime. First, they need to please the almighty to rescue themselves from punishment. After pleasing him, they perform their promise to the deity. They never dare to cheat God because they know the harder penalty than Sisyphus and his omniscient camera. Most of the holy texts have written about animal sacrifice; though rituals vary according to history, religion, culture, geography, and race.

Animals are beheaded when they are sacrificed. Before sacrificing, they sprinkle them with holy water, do some rituals, decorate, colour, add flowers, and even feed them. Sometimes they sprinkle with herbal perfume. The reason is, divinity doesn't accept dirty, wounded, spotted, unhealthy, undecorated, and ugly offerings.

Pigs, goats, buffalos, pigeons, ducks, fish, cocks, are sacrificed to various Shakti deities. Animals are not self-made they have been sacrificed by devotees. People named baby animals in the name of deities. Sometimes before the birth of an animal they gift to the Almighty. Sometimes people offer their unborn children to Deity.

Before birth, that baby becomes a scapegoat in the name of God, religion, culture, belief, and social status. A good example is Kumari system of Nepal. Why do we oblation? Because we expect, hope, desire, will, boon, blessing, and a gift from him. Pleasure, happiness, success, good health, prosperity, status, prestige, longevity, and glory are synonyms. Why does man sacrifice animals that animals don't do? Because animals don't have the fear and dread of means of subsistence, health, future, family, crisis, and dying. It is our reasoning that creates problems in relation to fear and death and dying. We have reason, knowledge, and rationale. We wish to save a life—our own from suffering with these negative emotions and thoughts.

These are simple examples. Anyone can be scapegoated at home, office, factory, society, and nation. Divorcees scapegoat their children. The heartless teachers scapegoats students. Rascal, toxic, bad offspring are scapegoated by parents and, may scapegoat parents. The quarrel of the board of directors scapegoats employees.

Corrupted presidents, ministers, political leaders and government employees scapegoat the public and the nation. The mistake of student A scapegoats student B. Notorious members of the political party scapegoat the whole party. Mistakes and deeds of one man scapegoat another. Knowingly or unknowingly, the game of scapegoating is everywhere.

Rene Girard criticizes sacrifice as the murder of a scapegoat that arrests the sacrificial crisis brought on by the contagion of mimetic desire [2].

THE MYTH OF SCAPEGOAT IN THE HOLY BIBLE

In the Bible, several places mention animal sacrifice. God required animal sacrifices to provide a temporary cleansing of sins and to foreshadow the perfect and complete sacrifice of Jesus Christ (Leviticus 4:35, 5:10).

Animal sacrifice is an important theme found throughout scripture because "without the shedding of blood there is no forgiveness" (Hebrews 9:22).

When Adam and Eve sinned, animals were killed by God to provide clothing for them (Genesis 3:21).

After the flood receded, Noah sacrificed animals to God (Genesis 8:20-21).

God commanded the nation of Israel to perform numerous sacrifices according to certain procedures prescribed by God. First, the animal had to be spotless. Second, the person offering the sacrifice had to identify with the animal. Third, the person offering the animal had to inflict death upon it. When done in faith, this sacrifice provided a temporary cleansing of sins. Another sacrifice called for on the Day of Atonement, described in Leviticus 16, demonstrates forgiveness and the removal of sin. The high priest was to take two male goats for a sin offering. One of the goats was sacrificed as a sin offering for the people of Israel (Leviticus 16:15), while the other goat was released into the wilderness (Leviticus 16:20-22).

The sin offering provided forgiveness, while the other goat provided the removal of sin. Why then, do we (Christians, especially) no longer offer animal sacrifices today? Animal sacrifices have ended because Jesus Christ was the ultimate and perfect sacrifice. John the Baptist recognized this when he saw Jesus coming to be baptized and said, "Look, the lamb of God who takes away the sin of the world" (John 1:29)!

Jesus Christ took our sins upon Himself and died in our place. As 2 Corinthians 5:21 says, "God made him [Jesus] who had no sin to be sin for us so that in him we might become the righteousness of God." Through faith in what Jesus Christ accomplished on the cross, we can receive forgiveness. In summation, animal sacrifices were commanded by God so that the individual could experience forgiveness of sin. The animal served as a substitute—that is, the animal died in place of the sinner, but only temporarily, which is why the sacrifices needed to be offered over and over. Animal sacrifices have stopped with Jesus Christ. Jesus Christ was the ultimate sacrificial substitute once for all time (Hebrews 7:27) and is now the only mediator between God and humanity (1 Timothy 2:5).

Animal sacrifices foreshadowed Christ's sacrifice on our behalf. The only basis on which an animal sacrifice could provide forgiveness of sins is Christ, who would sacrifice Himself for our sins, providing the forgiveness that animal sacrifices could only illustrate and foreshadow.

You may be asking yourself, why animals? What did they do wrong? That is the point—since the animals did no wrong, they died in place of the one performing the sacrifice. Jesus Christ also did no wrong but willingly gave Himself to die for the sins of mankind (1 Timothy 2:6) [3].

Patriots, martyrs, and leaders offer themselves for mankind, independence, liberty, freedom, democracy, communism, Nazism, fascism, identity, race, community, etc., the same as Jesus Christ. The form of sacrifice is invisible. In other words, we can say, invisible self-scapegoat. Every country and community has a long name list of it. The motive of their oblation is prosperity, happiness, good health, good education, a good future, long, and heavenly life. The sacrifice of animals, Jesus, and our patriot are guided by the same principle. It reminds people to sacrifice animals to achieve success, happiness, and good health.

Nelson Mandela (27 years) and Antonio Gramsci (20 years) spent long punishments in prison. Aung San Suu Kyi is still under house arrest. Mahatma Gandhi, Jawaharlal Nehru, and Subash Chandra Bose of India were jailed from time to time. South African and Indian leaders offered sacrifice of freedom for the country's independence. Suu Kyi is fighting for Democracy. Four famous patriots and martyrs of Nepal Shukraraj Shastri, Dharma Bhakta Mathema, Dashrath Chand, and Gangalal Shrestha were given the death penalty by the dictator Rana regime of Nepal. They were fighting for democracy. Their sacrifice was for the liberty of the people from cruel Rana rule. English civil war, the French Revolution, and the American Revolution scapegoated many Patriots and martyrs. Their hecatomb was for liberty. Occasionally several Patriots were house arrested, jailed, and killed. When we talk about history, history is written on the blood of contributors. The form of oblation varies but the objective is the same. The surrender of Socrates was also for mankind and philosophy.

First, animals were sacrificed to remove the sin of man. It was God's order. Later, Jesus offered himself on behalf of animals because animals were innocent. Those who disobeyed orders were sent to an inferno and given a boulder. The deity feared that if not punished, no one followed the order. In the same way, rulers, and colonizers were afraid of revolutionary forces, people, and leaders. Thus, they were sentenced many, or tortured, and jailed.

TRADITION AND CULTURE SCAPEGOAT

Chander P. Maharjan writes an article about animal sacrifice as the ritual killing and offering of an animal usually as part of a religious appeasement of a deity. A Sanskrit term used for animal sacrifice is *bali*, in origin meaning "tribute, offering or oblation."

Birds are usually the animals used in sacrifice rituals, but there can also be a goat, sheep, chickens, pigs, dogs, little guinea pigs, turtles-fish, crabs, doves, ducks, elephants, horses, ox, bulls, camel, cow, Ram, pigeons; and the massive ones were all being sacrificed.

Fowl, chicken, goat-lamb, child pig–pig, sheep; each would be the best specimen of its kind, cleansed, clad in sacrificial regalia, and garlanded-the horns of oxen might be gilded. Black rooster has been more common. The rams have been sought after. Even blood, oozing out of cockfights is considered appropriate.

In the Indonesian island of Bali, the religious belief of Tabuh Rah, a form of animal sacrifice, includes a cockfight. The spilling of blood is necessary as purification to appease evil spirits. In the Indian state of Kerala cockfighting is a religious exercise of offering blood to the Theyyam gods.

Israelites believed that sacrifice was a necessary part of the relationship between God and man. Animal sacrifices were common throughout Europe and continue in some cultures and religions today.

In Meghalaya, at Nongkrem Dance festival, the High priest offers oblation to the god of Shyllong peak by sacrificing a cock. An important part of this festival is Pemblang (sacrifice of goats). Colorful banners of Cock Sacrifice is a common sight.

Mong Greeks blood sacrifices were divided into burnt offerings in which the whole unmaimed animal was burnt (holocaust), guilt offerings (in which part was burnt and partly left for the priest), and peace offerings (in which only part of the undamaged animal was burnt and the rest eaten in ritually pure conditions).

Sacrifices are performed for life events such as birth, marriage, and death. They are also used for healing. Without sacrifice the religion would die out, and, therefore, sacrifice is essential for initiation into the faith in the community and the satisfaction of priests.

According to Walter Burkert, a scholar of sacrifice, Greek sacrifices derived from hunting practices. Hunters, feeling guilty for having killed another living being so they could eat and survive, tried to repudiate their responsibility in these rituals. According to one school of thought, the animal is sacrificed as food, rather than for any obscure mystical purpose.

Sacrifices could include bloodless offerings (grain and wine), the animal sacrifices were considered the most important by many.

In the past, animal sacrifice was practiced at the ancient Shakti temple, Bahu Fort (3000 years old), in the city of Jammu, which has since been discontinued. Today, a priest performs a few rites uttering some religious incantations and sprinkles holy water over the animal (usually a sheep or goat), and then lets it go free [4].

Jesus Christ also did no wrong but willingly gave himself to die for the sins of mankind (1 Timothy 2:6). In The Bible verses, Jesus offers himself on behalf of animals. His offering was not beyond the scapegoat. It was self-made.

At present, scapegoats can be seen in all kinds of markets. Forms are distinct but nature is similar. I have referenced it to show in multidisciplinary studies. It can be studied in the political, social, religious, economic, traditional, cultural, and labor scapegoats. I categorize them as direct, indirect, general, special, and other scapegoats.

1. Direct scapegoat

A. Personally- a person offers himself as Jesus did in Timothy 2:6. Jesus offered on behalf of animals. A man offers for his benefits. It is a self-made sacrifice and offer. They want to be a success, happy, and prosperous, and thus, prepares and offers to the employer, customer, and audience; wears smart dresses, and makeup, do fitness, exercise, and looks sharp. Many employees come into this category. To find a good job, they get a higher degree, good knowledge, and keep smart. They hope once they succeed in life they will be set. They are not sacrificed by others, they offer themselves.

B. Political, spiritual, and motivational- leaders always get ready for the best performance, speech, and motivation. To draw public attention, they practice, read, and do social work. They do it for desires. They oblate themselves to the audience. They are self-made Jesus-type scapegoats.

2. Indirect Scapegoat

Most people are not self-made scapegoats. They are made by other people. Animals and human sacrifice come under this category. Noah sacrificed animals to God after the flood receded (Genesis 8:20-21).

A man plays the agent role. Through them, the animal is sacrificed. In the past, superstitions, religions, politics, economics, and blind beliefs practiced it. They garlanded, prepared, decorated, fed, and kept the animal healthy because the almighty didn't accept unbaptized animals. They must be a good look. A devotee does good care of God-named animals. Once the deity accepts the tribute the project will be fruitful, and the enemies will end. It is their belief.

In Nepal, the concept of Kumari Goddess (living Goddess) is popular and still operating. They are believed as living Goddesses. Kumari means virgin and considered as holiest. Sacrifices are to them, that is, to Taleju or Durga Goddess. Many tourists come to visit them. Kathmandu, Lalitpur, and Bhaktapur have living Kumaris. Once they became living Goddesses, they have been forbidden to marry and live unmarried life. If they marry, their husband will die, it is a religious belief.

Such traditions and cultures we find in many countries. They are not self-made; they have been made by cultural tradition and belief. The main objective of this belief is prosperity, happiness, forgiveness, removal of sin, and success in life, family, community, and nation.

3. Other

We have many other kinds of scapegoats in our society. We rarely notice them.

Political Scapegoat

Some political leaders are self-made and some are made by others. They want to lead the community and nation. Sometimes they appear directly and sometimes indirectly. They learn and practice, are well-dressed, and do good performances in mass meetings and rallies. Sometimes, the high command of the party sacrifices them. They offer their candidacy for the nation.

We can see many scapegoats in politics. Political leaders make civilians direct and indirect scapegoats. High command or party decides whom to sacrifice. Even high command becomes self-made. Patriots and martyrs are self-made. Suu Kyi is under house arrest. Mostly dictator makes their civilians victims. The military rule of Myanmar and other countries makes scapegoats for people.

At present, we can see scapegoat civilians in the Ukraine war. Lots of wars and revolutions have been happening in the world.

Many innocents become victims. Hitler sacrificed innocent Jews (Holocaust). The first World War, second World War, Cold War, Vietnam War, and Korean War scapegoated many people. Some were for the personal benefit of the ruler, and some were for the national interest. The ego, prestige, love, and hate of the ruler killed many of them.

Troy, Mahabharat, and Ramayana War massacred masses of people. The first public, second ruler, and third enemies became victimgoats. Many were imprisoned in the name of war crimes.

In the past, slaves were scapegoated. During the Nazi, Mussolini, Stalin, and Pol Pot's rules, many civilians were killed. Japan scapegoated several Chinese and non-Chinese. Million war victimgoats were in the past and millions are living in the present.

Every day we see thousands of refugees crossing borders carrying luggage, and baby. Some of them have been devoured by starvation, desert, river, sea, and forest. Innumerable disabled, injured, blind, deaf, crippled, handicapped, maimed, paralyzed, impaired, wounded, lamed, feeble, orphan, poor, and mental are left behind. They are just obliterated.

Major characters of Kafka's story and novel are victims of culture, belief, and morality. In his writing, we can see atrocity and torture but we cannot see the monster of atrocity. Between torturer and atrocity, the innocent becomes the scapegoat. Kafka is an example.

Religious and Cultural Scapegoats

During the medieval era, a large number of people had been victimized. The Dark Ages was the Age of Scapegoats in the name of God and religion. The priest and ruler benefited but they sacrificed uncountable lives.

Socrates, Aristotle, Galileo, Giordano Bruno, Anna Frank, Thomas Hobbes, Karl Marx, Jean-Paul Sartre, Kafka's three sisters, and innumerable innocents were victimized. Socrates, Marx, Aristotle, and Hitler are victims of political, religious, and moral problems. Socrates, Gregor Samsa and Georg Bendemann were unfairly scapegoated. Hitler's case is unique. He dug his inferno and was buried there. He offered his candidacy himself.

The Cultural Revolution of China and the Communist rule of Russia scapegoated people, religion, culture, language, and lives. It did not happen in the interest of the public; it happened in the interest of a handful of men. Of their selfishness, poor citizens became the victims. Even today, we can see many countries, killing each other in the name of belief, blind belief, language, race, culture, superstition, and identity. They don't know the Chakravyuh (squared planning). Entrapped are scapegoats indeed. Victims don't know they are in a trap. It is a Super Scapegoat Structure (SSS).

Spiritual leaders, motivational speakers, priests, bishops, and pastors, garland, get ready, tidy, clean, spotless, healthy, smart, and makeup like sacrificial animals. They prepare for a good appearance. If their appearance and presentation are not good, the masses don't accept them. Their appearance is self-made, but they sacrifice others on their behalf. In the name of culture and religion, several widows were scapegoated by SSS in Sati System.

It has General Scapegoat Structure (GSS) and Super Scapegoat Structure (SSS). GSS is a direct way of scapegoating and SSS is a special way of scapegoating. The superstructure of Marxism and the cultural hegemony of Antonio Gramsci is SSS. People cannot accept severe scapegoating for a long time. When they know it, they revolt. So, higher-class people create a less visible web in SSS. For example, if people scapegoat through religion, culture, custom, belief, and deity, they sincerely become the scapegoat and never mind against it. A newly born baby is a scapegoat of desire, believe and prestige of parents. They don't born by their desire. After birth, they face many crisis in the life.

Capitalist Scapegoat

In capitalism, in front of the customer, in production, marketing, company, and sale, they offer and sacrifice themselves. We can take a salesman, customer service, agent, broker, labour, the proletariat, representative, executive director, chairman, manager, and CEO as participants. At present most capitalist holds the CEO post. When they do business deals, contracts, and launch projects, they decorate themselves as offering to God. Their God is client, customer, and business partner. In marketing, one famous slogan is, "Customer is always right." In the case of an employee, "The boss is always right." For theologists, "God is always right." They become tidy, hygienic, and smart to offer skill, expertise, talent, and professionalism. For it, the makeup, training, and dressing room are made. Those rooms sprinkle water, making them holy and spotless. We can see Mr. Samsa in this all. He, how well dressed up when he prepared to go to work.

Why I inserted capitalists in the scapegoat because they offer their projects. To get success they prepare smartness, tidiness, fitness, cleverness, good performance, and the use of government and agents. Capitalists have many levels. They use others as a scapegoat, and sometimes themselves. The big uses the small as a scapegoat. The biggest is self-made.

Suppose, a capitalist, launches a product, then just before launch, they decorate themselves, make themselves showy and handsome, and good look. They may hire other companies. Sometimes buys other companies. The product and brand represent them. In the name of the product, and the brand they offer, and that they are the foundation for the symbolic and real sacrifice of themselves. They scapegoat others to roll their freight to the mountain-top.

The scapegoat is everywhere, sometimes romantic, and sometimes thriller. Chinese and American trade wars made many scapegoats. Huawei mobile and its chips were the issues once. Chinese mobile companies became scapegoats in the Western world. In this case, the direct victim was Meng Wanzhou of Huawei. She was arrested in Canada. Mobile phones, McDonald, KFC, shoe companies, car companies, and dress companies become scapegoats from time to time. Sometimes they scapegoat others and sometimes they become themselves. Megalothymia, asserted Francis Fukuyama, is applicable. Every country and individual wants to be superior to others.

To achieve the goal, they scapegoated lots of *Antonio (es). Recently, Elon Musk scapegoated many employees. In the development competition many employees and the public, become victims. It is the nature of multinational businesses. Before going to market, they prepare a strategy for the best design, decoration, promotion, and skill like an animal is being taken to sacrifice.

The collapse of American banks scapegoated employees and customers. The sacrificial animals receive a sprinkle with holy water, and are decorated with colours. It is ritual at core. In a capitalist world, decoration and promotion are their baptisms. They are afraid that if not sprinkled with promotional materials, they might be rejected in the market. One sees through a fearist lens the foundations in even the secular Capitalist world so-called, the religious is operating, the fear and superstition, the taboos and the conformism. Few risk to authentically raise this observation to theory and alternative practices.

Employee Scapegoat

When British rule was in India, Nepalese boys were recruited into the army as Gurkha soldiers. Even today, they recruit them into the British, Indian, and Singapore police. At the time of recruitment, they check, height, weight, chest, and health and take some exams. If they were fit, they were signed up and sent to war on behalf of the British. The rejected of them were sent back home. This is a process of recruiting the army and police everywhere. Almost similar recruitment happens for every employee. Only forms and models differ.

Any job seeker when going to find a job, first physically gets ready. He takes a bath, wears a tidy dress, sprinkles perfumes, combs hair, and polishes shoes. He prepares mentally, for an interview, exam, discussion, or present project.

If somebody wants to join some games; parents, coaches, and teachers make them ready. They feed them nutritious meals and let them do physical exercise. They do it for a better look and physical fitness. As much as for employees, they want to get a degree, skill, knowledge, and language and make more money. Those who have more degrees, skills, and experiences, can have more chances to be accepted. All these are like a scapegoating process.

At present, competition is high. Selected candidates are the best scapegoat. They metamorphose for good jobs, good designation, opportunities, and high salaries. Animals and many sacrifices are a bit different, but the meaning is the same. The scapegoat word is a little degraded, but it is an outlook of labour and the capitalist market.

An employee offers to please the employer and customer. When they are pleased, he can fulfill his desires as a devotee does. He gets a promotion, bonus, status and commission.

We are in Sotalism Age. Employees are one kind of self-made scapegoat. They offer themselves, as mentioned earlier, *via* direct scapegoat. No one has ordered them to be so. Many types of fears are behind their offering and sacrifice.

The nature of Sisyphus and Bhageeratha is mismatched. We can find levels of employees playing this out. Suppose A is a security guard in a company. B is the management company. C is the owner of a building. A recruits security guard. B hires them. C is the buyer. First C hires management and management hires a guard for C. So, the guard becomes a hand-to-hand saleable human commodity. A makes a 1st-grade scapegoat, and later it sells them to other companies, which is a 2nd-grade scapegoat. Sometimes it goes to 3rd, and 4th grade too.

The slaves were similar scapegoats. This kind of hiring is in the bank, financial company, military, police, etc. Whether manpower companies or other companies, the scapegoat form makes a 'good' business. Human and refugee trafficking are the same. Selling and buying slaves were very traditional. The refugee and human trafficking business are fostered in a Trans Philosophism era. It is a big business. Big areas of the market are covered by it. In containers, human freight is illegally exported and imported.

Animal and employee sacrifice have similarities and dissimilarities. We offer animals to God. An animal's life is sacrificed. Either animal or employee, man benefited. Employees are front-line scapegoats. In the 19th century labour, worker, and proletariat words were popular. In the 21st century, the employee word is popular.

Multinational Scapegoat

Multinational companies buy small companies and use them as Antonio. Antonio became almost a scapegoat by his best friend Bassanio. International banks scapegoat for national and local banks. Starbucks coffee scapegoats for local coffee shops.

At present, we can see many such businesses in the international market. Many brands, trademarks, manufacturing, delivery, distributor, supermarkets, Malls, and agents are in this business. The tourist industry is rapidly spreading all over the world.

Almost 75% of tourist industries scapegoat nature. To handle these brands, banks, financial institutions, insurance companies, and governments involved. Some multinational companies are self-made and some are made by others.

Ecological Scapegoat

In the name of capitalism, development, colonization, and wars, we are not scapegoating only civilians, we are scapegoating nature, ecology, and the environment. Air pollution and poisoning water are our contributions.

We decorate nature, ecology, and the environment in the name of plantation, greenery, and conservation. UN and nations spend huge budgets for environmental protection, conservation, and preservation.

It is like sprinkling water and decoration on a black rooster before sacrifice. Later, sacrifice, slash, and eat. We are cruel to the ecology. Some parts of ecology are dying, and some parts have already died.

In reverse, nature is taking revenge, it scapegoated us. Who is responsible for Australia and Amazon fires? Who is answerable for flooding, global warming, and drought in Europe and America? The beautiful forest, river, sea, wetland, animal, mountain, air, land, and desert became the scapegoat.

Eight billion people are at the bottom of all these crises. Nature is crying, moaning, and looking for help. We are pitilessly killing. We are not murdering ecology, but we are destroying to earth and sky with human bombs.

The planets and stars are in our range. War, industrial development, road, urbanization, reclamation, and capitalism are liable for it. We accept spotless ecology, but we spotted its Cleopatra face.

Many marks and dots are in the environment. Now we have less beautiful and more scary nature. The spotted ecology is the boon of human bombs. The ecology is injured, handicapped, maimed, paralyzed, impaired, wounded, and lamed. It is crawling, creeping like insect Gregor Samsa.

Two schools of thought have been developing in Panopticon on ecology.

1. Eco-Philosophy of Fearism

In this camp, R. Michael Fisher has written on "Eco-Philosophy of fearism and ecocriticism: In an Age of Terror." He says, "We [humanity] have a fear of global warming, pollution, an increase of mass destruction weapons" [5].

2. Eco-Fearism

Dr. Bhawani Shankar Adhikari, Osinakachi Akuma Kalu, and Desh Subba have written the book *Eco-Fearism: Prospective &*

Burning Issues. Adhikari writes in his book Yarshagumbaism (2022), "The policies are to be made by the joint pressure of all the nations. So the superpower nations along with the information of the global degradation of eco-condition. If the entire nations of the globe come in one place, then it becomes true. No other systems function in a normal form sans the sound ecosystem. Political pressure groups and the experts' suggestions must be addressed by the superpower nations. The UNO must initiate it so far, the autonomous of them on time since it is being delayed" [6].

These are camps of Philosophy of Fearism. Many sub-camps may rise in the near future.

Piergiacomo Severini writes, "Fearism and Eco-Fearism want to give expression to the unexpressed experienced in day to day affairs of life, developing a contextualist ethical philosophy that gives back importance to the human condition, its goals, its capabilities"[7].

Yuval Noah Harari writes, "Perhaps if more people were aware of the first-wave and second-wave extinctions they'd be less nonchalant about the third wave they are part of. If we know how many species we've already eradicated, we might be more motivated to protect those that still survive. this is especially relevant to the large animal of the oceans" [8].

Muhammad Iqbal, mentions, "The Philosophy of Fearism is an interdisciplinary approach that can be applied to various areas of human life and society. Eco-Fearism, for example, focuses on the role of fear in shaping our relationship with the environment and how we can transform fear into positive action to address ecological crises" [9].

The history of colonization and capitalism is a history of scapegoats. Those are not only scapegoats, those are victimgoats.

The most of hegemony, orientalism, marginal, colonized, and subaltern are scapegoats. In war, colonization, culture, language, and belief we're victimized.

For the ego, selfishness, greed, love, and desire made many scapegoats. Animals, plants, and nature to men became victims of war, ego, love, and colonization. The colonizer scapegoated, man, animal, ecology, culture, language, literature, music, and nation.

History, art, culture, literature, philosophy, and criticism must rewrite from a victimgoat point of view because it is a true story and no one has written them. It is their right. History put them out of right and justice.

What doctrine we have today is the doctrine of injustice and false. It is a time to rewrite doctrine for those who were victimized. Their original history is shadowed. Victimgoat or victim+goat is more appropriate than scapegoat or scape+goat because those were victimized. Scapegoats are semi and victimgoats are full scapegoats. Victimgoat studies are necessary. The area of the subaltern, hegemony, and refugee studies is smaller than victimgoat. Victimgoat studies were concealed by the superstructure concept of Marx. Subaltern, marginal, and hegemony—it can be overturned by victimgoat theory.

If we see the second Geneva Convention of 1929, which was for prisons of war, and the fourth Convention of 1949, which was for civilians. The first Geneva Convention of 1863 was for war victim soldiers. All Geneva Conventions are for the victims. We have many conventions, treaties, and laws for a scapegoat but these are overshadowed and are not disclosed. Trans Philosophism is the best time for disclosing them.

HIERARCHY OF SCAPEGOAT

The weaker, poor, and small companies always become scapegoats. In other words, it has a *hierarchy of fear*. In the Sati system, the widow always became a scapegoat. Sati is a Hindu practice, in which a widow sacrifices herself by sitting atop her deceased husband's funeral pyre. Can we say it is herself? Does any widow want to sit in her deceased husband's pyre?

Most of the scapegoats are lower from the top. Widow's status is weak in society, she easily becomes the scapegoat. Although, any rich, powerful and upper-class widow can be the scapegoat? Widows had first, culture and religion fear, and second self-immolation. It was SSS. She could not escape because a crowd of strong men imprisons her. She had been forced to sit in her deceased husband's pyre. If she goes front, she will kill by the dogmatic public, if she goes to the pyre, she will burn by fire, she chooses the fire. She must immolate.

It was not self-immolation. Why could society not sacrifice a widower? Because a woman has no power. Victims of Kafkaesque are weak in power. Why did Mr. Samsa, the Father of Georg and Hermann Kafka not scapegoated? The answer is they had power. Rules and regulations were made by them. Likewise lower caste, subaltern, colonize, refugee, female, migrant, hegemonize, and marginal people always be scapegoated.

A slave cannot scapegoat his master. The animal cannot make a scapegoat for a man. Devotees cannot scapegoat God. The scapegoats are always slaughtered by the rich, ruler, capitalist, bourgeois, male, priest, and father. Then, who slaughters them? Their structures are self-made. The cause of their chopping is their ego, jealousy, selfishness, greediness, hate, love, and fear.

There is a common ground for scapegoats that is a good job, success, happiness, a bright future, good health, peace, prestige, reputation, forgiveness, and social status. The benefit of a scapegoat always is employed by the capitalist, the ruler, the bourgeois, the male, the employer, the priest, the father, and the upper class. They are engineers of SSS.

The lower class becomes a scapegoat. They want to be saved from known or unknown fears. In Bible, they sacrifice animals to remove sin and for forgiveness. To meet the target, sometimes they sacrifice themselves, and sometimes forcibly sacrifice others. These are some instances. If we see from the scapegoat, we are scapegoat animals. The SSS is made by higher people to lower. Fear (spirit) is at the top of all in this hierarchy.

ABOUT THE THEORY OF
THE SCAPEGOAT

Ashley Crossman writes about the theory of scapegoat, scapegoating refers to a process by which a person or group is unfairly blamed for something that they didn't do and, as a result, the real source of the problem is either never seen or purposefully ignored. Sociologists have documented that scapegoating often occurs between groups when a society is plagued by long-term economic problems or when resources are scarce. Scapegoat theory is used in sociology and psychology as one way to intercept conflict and prejudice between individuals and groups.

The term scapegoat has Biblical origins, coming from the Book of Leviticus. In the book, a goat was sent into the desert carrying the sins of the community. So, a scapegoat was originally understood as a person or animal that symbolically absorbed the sins of others and carried them away from those who committed them.

Scapegoating also occurs in a one-on-group manner, when one person blames a group for a problem they did not cause: wars, deaths, financial losses of one kind or another, and other personal struggles. This form of scapegoating may sometimes be unfairly blamed on racial, ethnic, religious, class, or anti-immigrant biases.

Finally, and of most interest to sociologists, is the form of scapegoating that is "group-on-group." This occurs when one group blames another for problems that the groups collectively experience, which might be economic or political in nature—like blaming a particular party for the Great Depression (1929-1939) or the Great Recession (2007-2009). This form of scapegoating often manifests across lines of race, ethnicity, religion, or national origin.

Scapegoating of one group by another has been used throughout history, and still today, as a way to incorrectly explain why certain social, economic, or political problems exist and harm the group doing the scapegoating. Some sociologists say that their research shows that groups that scapegoat occupy a low socio-economic status in society and have little access to wealth and power. They say these people are often experiencing prolonged economic insecurity or poverty, and come to adopt shared outlooks and beliefs that have been documented to lead to prejudice and violence.

Sociologists who embrace socialism as a political and economic theory argue that those in a low socioeconomic status are naturally inclined to scapegoat due to the unequal distribution of resources within the society. These sociologists place blame on capitalism as an economic model and exploitation of workers by a wealthy minority. However, these are not the viewpoints of all sociologists. As with any science involving theories, study, research, and conclusions—it's not an exact science, and therefore there will be a variety of viewpoints [10].

Crossman's writing hints of the hierarchy of fear. Low socioeconomic status is easily scapegoated. Gregor Samsa is the best paradigm. Most of the Gregors are homogeneously scapegoated. We pay less attention to them. General knowledge of scapegoat we can get from it. More theoretical analysis has to be done and shape it to interdisciplinary studies level.

SCAPEGOAT REASONING

We know the reason for the scapegoat in Troy, Mahabharata, and Ramayana. Why did Antonio become the scapegoat between Shylock and Bassanio? Why did Socrates scapegoat? Why was Sisyphus victimized? The condition of Socrates and Sisyphus was under SSS. We can find many scapegoat characters in fiction and reality shows of life. We never notice them. My focus is on capitalism on the basis of Das Capital. How were labourers scapegoated to heave up capital?

Scapegoat is a soft word for exploitation. The first reason for it is the means of subsistence. Other reasons are happiness, pleasure, success, benefit, facilities, ego, love, and glory. It is applicable to capitalism, an employer, or an employee. Slowly, people metamorphose into different classes, groups, and teams. When they reach the profit-making stage, the scapegoat is played more extremist. Profit doesn't merely mean economic, it can apply to all means of facilitation of life. For profit, emerges various scapegoats. Somebody was happy to make a scapegoat and somebody was victimized.

Capitalism uses scapegoats in multiple ways. Basically, we are discussing here fearmorphosis views.

Such an ideal workhouse must be made a "House of Terror," and not an asylum for the poor, "Where they are to be plentifully fed, warmly and decently clothed, and where they do but little work." In this, "House of Terror," this "ideal workhouse, the poor shall work 14 hours in a day, allowing proper time for meals, in such manner that there shall remain 12 hours of neat-labour [11].

The House of Terror was actually the "House of Scapegoat". It was made to feed and clothe workers. They were to be plentifully fed, warmly and decently clothed, allowing them proper time for a meal and taking them to do 14 hours of work. At present, the form of the 'House of Scapegoat' has changed. They are allowing air conditioning room, tie and suit, good dress and given the best training. This preparation is for commission, profit, and attracting customers.

The "House of Terror" for paupers which the capitalistic soul of 1770 only dreamed of, was realized a few years later in the shape of a gigantic "Workhouse" for the industrial worker himself [12].

The "House of Terror" was later promoted to a gigantic "Workhouse'. It means house of scapegoat resized. Does the scapegoat have a choice? No, just sacrifice. Industrial workers were dancing according to the capitalist music. The present employees enjoy high rises and multistore buildings.

Previously, the workman sold his own labour-power, which he disposed of nominally as a free agent. Now he sells his wife and child [13].

Workman was first a self-made scapegoat. Later, he scapegoated his wife and child to protect his life. He offered and sacrificed them. It was very pitiable and miserable. No one sold himself, his wife, and his child until fear didn't appear.

Suppose one side is the workman, his wife, and his child, on contrary, is fear. When he was able to maintain a family he didn't need to sell anyone. In the above situation, the workman sold labour-power first, to protect his family, but at last, he sold his wife and child to protect himself. How dear to the family, it didn't matter he wanted to save his life. Gregor Samsa was very dear to his mother and sister. When he transformed into vermin, their dearest terminated.

As the use of machinery becomes more general in a particular industry, the social value of products inks down to their individual value, and the law that surplus-value doesn't arise from the labour-power that has been replaced by the machinery, but from the labour-power actually employed in working with the machinery, with asserts itself [14].

After the entrance of machinery, the labour-value was scapegoated. It snatched and kick off them, as is Marx's belief. In this condition, they could be fitted to some other fields. At present, advanced machines used in production but a huge population is engaged in different fields. A good model is, in Nepal, a bus has three staff; a driver, conductor, and helper. In developed countries, all work is done by a driver. The rest of the two staff employ some other fields.

Many of them died of starvation, many with families vegetated for a long time on two and half a day [15] .

Labours had always high risk. Risk is similar to the boulder that was above the Sisyphus. At any time chances to fall down. Many proletariat Sisyphus lost their jobs. They vegetated for a long time two and half a days. Either capitalist or worker, means of livelihood was the cause. It can be read in Samsa's family. Death was the last termination. An unsafe situation was there in London. Many effort manvs were in London and the rest of the world.

According to Gaskell, the steam-engine was from the very first an antagonist of human power, an antagonist, that enabled the capitalist to tread underfoot the growing claims of the workmen, who threatened the newly born factory system with a crisis [16].

Gaskell believed the steam engine was the antagonist of human power. For the capitalist, it was one step up toward the mountain-top. Workmen's life was on high alert.

Suppose Arjun is ready to play Conch in the Kurukshetra war. 18 days war was an important part of Mahabharat like Troy. Gaskell's belief was Karl Marx's beliefs. Indeed, the steam engine was the advancement of technology. It facilitated human life. Of course, it scapegoated certain groups.

For the present I will only say this: The labourers that are thrown out of work in any branch of industry, can no doubt seek employment in some other branch [17].

First, the labourers were thrown out of work, and it was done by a steam engine. So, they needed alternative means of subsistence.

Agriculture came as an alternative to hunting and industry came as the development of agriculture. In the 21st-century capitalist system, workers were thrown out of work for any reason. Reasons might be the economic crisis, war, insolvency of the company, bankruptcy, and natural problems. The employees needed to roll a new stone as means of subsistence.

So soon as machinery sets free a part of the workmen employed in a given branch of industry, the reserve men are also diverted into new channels of employment, and become absorbed in other branches; meanwhile the original victims, during the period of transition, for the most part starve and perish [18].

The transition period is always in life. If we see the life of Sisyphus and Bhageeratha their life is also in this period. At that moment, as soon as machinery set free a part of the workmen employed in each branch of industry, the reserve men were also diverted into new channels of employment. Unfortunately, the original workmen were victimized.

The machinery and steam engine were the biggest achievement in civilization. Meantime, it was a great threat to the workmen. At present, many challenges are on the way like population, unemployment, pollution, global warming, war, terrorism, financial crisis, nuclear, drought, and fall of capital. Consequently, it scapegoats many people and takes them to hell.

B. Maria Kumar and B. S. Sushmita write, As Karl Marx equated work with life, an unhealthy man cannot enjoy his work. Rather he cannot work. Sickness, laziness, slackness, inertness, immobility, bed-riddenness, narrow-mindedness, blockade of mind, lethargy, etc., interfere with work, thereby causing not only an injustice to work but also inconvenience and discomfort to the people who are around [19].

SCAPEGOATED NATURE

Michael Bassey Eneyo writes, "We sand-fill the sea to build houses and in the name of development, we produce chemicals that kill the grasses. Inventions of these dangerous chemicals and other disastrous apparatuses are on the rise by the day. By so doing, we destroy the nutrients in the soil with these chemicals and terminate lives through the dangerous weapons introduced by us" [20].

We scapegoated the soil, forest, animal, river, sky, land, and air to heave up society, civilization, agriculture, industry, and capital. Consequently, fertile land, air, and forests are converted into infertile. We transformed beautiful earth into hell. Infertile soil, air, and greenery scapegoat man because the fertility of soil dies. Infertile land produces less product and sometimes does not. The first humans scapegoated fertile land, air, water, forest, and infertile land, water, air, and forest scapegoated man. It is a tit-for-tat. The transformer of this inferno is not by other people. We dug it. If we go to see the hell of No Exit, Karma was the cause of hell.

This fertile soil was transformed into infertile soil by rapacious methods of cultivation, and now the soil of Michigan appeared as the more fertile [21]. It is an important matter for farmers. Farmers are the basis of agricultural countries. The fertile soil was transfigured into infertile by rapacious methods of cultivation. Man scapegoated for his use. It was dangerous for everyone. When it became normal, the fear of being infertile was over but it had fewer chances. Infertile soil ended in Michigan at that time, but it is more treacherous now.

The use of different types of chemicals is increasing very fast all over the world. Just for the time being, it produces crops. Its toxicity destroys the soil, and gradually the economy of the country dies. When we produce toxic crops, it slowly kills us. We are almost in the danger zone. We are designers, makers, and victims of scapegoats. First, we dig a graveyard for nature, and later, we bury ourselves in this hell.

This rent is distinguished, in the first place, by the preponderant influence exerted here by location upon differential rent (very significant, e.g., in the vineyard and building sites in large cities); secondly, by the palpable and complete passiveness of the owner, whose sole activity consists (especially in mines) in exploiting the progress of social development, towards which he contributes nothing and for which he risks nothing, unlike the industrial capitalist; and finally by the prevalence of monopoly prices in many cases, particularly through the most shameless exploitation of poverty (for poverty is more lucrative for house-rent than the mines of Potost ever were for Spain), and the monstrous power wielded by the landed property, when united hand and hand with industrial capital, enables it to be used against labourers engaged in their wage struggle as a means of practically expelling them from the earth as a dwelling-place [22].

Marx criticized the rent system and said in exploiting the progress of social development, towards which he contributes nothing and for which he risks nothing, unlike the industrial capitalist; and finally by the prevalence of monopoly prices in many cases, particularly through the most shameless exploitation of poverty, and the monstrous power wielded by the landed property, when united hand and hand with industrial capital, enables it to be used against labourers engaged in their wage struggle as a means of practically expelling them from the earth as a dwelling-place. It is part of capitalism and capitalism is a part of human development. Hunting and agriculture solved the food crisis. Every step of development carries a package of Pandora. Capitalism and Marxism cannot ignore it because it is a part of life. The absence of it is noumena (Xfearomenon). Marx indicated rent was against labourers and it must be eradicated. Kill a Shylock mind was his point. Some of his accusations are baseless because they have some contributions and risks for investments.

Two elements should be considered here: on the one hand, the exploitation of the earth for the purpose of reproduction or extraction; on the other hand; the space required as an element of all production and all human activity [23].

We have in detail explained such things in Eco-Fearism and Eco-Philosophy of Fearism. In the name of the production, raw material, and extraction, we scapegoated the earth. Its main causing factor is the growing population. A large population requires more land, water, oxygen, housing, road, industry, production, and capital. What we are doing, its effect goes to nature, and it reflects tit for tat. Global warming, pollution, drought, and melting ice are reflections of our Karma. It is called Karma Ko Fall, which means Gathering thistles & expecting pickles in English. We are Eris of ecological crises. We grave ourselves in the netherworld.

In the same way, the slave-holder considers an African (once called Negro), whom he has purchased, as his property, not because the institution of slavery as much entitles him to that African, but because he has acquired him like any other commodity, through sale and purchase [24].

The slaves were taken as commodities. Their form was a scapegoat. Why were Negros scapegoated? Were they self-made? The scapegoat concept was not highlighted by Marx and postmodernism thinkers whereas Marxism and postmodernism are shadow theories of scapegoat. Some of them were self-made and some of them were made by others. They served their whole life to the buyer. They were like Homer's underworld Sisyphus. If they had power, they were never sold, bought, scapegoated, and made cage Sisyphus. Slave-holders were Shylocks.

Rather than tracing to their origin the real natural causes leading to an exhaustion of the soil, which, incidentally, were unknown to all economists writing on differential rent owing to the level of agricultural chemistry in their day, the swallow conception was seized upon that any amount of capital cannot be invested in a limited area of land; as the *Edinburgh Review*, [Tome LIV, August-December 1831, pp. 94-95.— Ed.] for instance, argued against Richard Jones that all of England cannot be fed through the cultivation of Soho Square [25].

Argument against Richard Jones was practical, all of England could not be fed through the cultivation of Soho Square. It was the picture of contemporary England. The population was increasing and feeding them through the cultivation of Soho Square, was not enough. The soil was limited and exhausted. The room was small as in No Exit, and that's why it became hell for others.

The earth is going to be a netherworld for us. As the Edinburgh review, any amount of capital could not be invested in a limited area, it required new land for the new population. In time, if they didn't take serious action people would suffer from famine. It was the reason, they marched into colonization.

If productivity rapidly developed, all of the old machinery must be replaced by the more advantageous; in other words, it is lost [26]. Productivity depends on the demand for the product. In England, demand was increasing, and to meet it, productivity rapidly developed. The productivity of the old machinery was slow to meet demand. So, it was replaced by more advantageous machines. In competition, must have high-quality and productive machinery. Which factory couldn't run in the race, it would be lost. At present, everything is controlled by a computer. To meet market demand, the latest version of the technology is necessary.

End Notes

1. https://phimag.org/blog/trans-philosophism-a-review
2. From Mahajan (2020).
3. https://churchlifejournal.nd.edu/articles/the-sacrifice-of-praise-and-animal-sacrifice/
4. https://www.gotquestions.org/animal-sacrifices.html
5. Mahajan (2020).
6. Adhikari (2020), p. 107.

7. https://www.academia.edu/50101597/Eco_Fearism_Review
8. Adhikari, Kalu and Subba (2020), p. 99.
9. https://fearlessnessmovement.ning.com/blog/the-philosophy-of-fearism-a-thought-provoking-perspective-on-fear?fbclid=IwAR0PwhUXzZM_um_LbacWJTUxt7xtQl_nQQK9CblHyYbLAG3xNgpiEXSEN8Y
10. https://www.thoughtco.com/scapegoat-definition-3026572
11. Marx (1998/2021), p. 169.
12. Ibid., p. 170.
13. Ibid., p. 254.
14. Ibid., p. 259.
15. Ibid., p. 270.
16. Ibid., p. 272.
17. Ibid., p. 274.
18. Ibid.
19. Kumar and Sushmita (2018), p. 141.
20. Eneyo (2018), p. 199.
21. Marx (1998/2021), p. 1237.
22. Ibid., p. 1311.
23. Ibid., p. 1312.
24. Ibid., p. 1311-12.
25. Ibid., p. 1315.
26. Ibid., p. 1315-16.

PART FOUR

CAPITAL

STORY OF *DAS CAPITAL*

The story of *Das Capital* is a Panopticon of Karl Marx. The fearists have been applying Fearism in philosophy, literature, education, healthcare, criticism, politics, ecology, and linguistics, but usually never apply it re: capital. It is a capital perspective doctrine we ought to challenge. Das Capital has less about capitalism and more about the labourer's crisis. Labourers are human beings. Therefore, better to say human capital.

Now, we can see fearmorphosis in Das Capital. Suppose all our emotions are at rest. Abruptly, an Echidna appeared. Among emotions, which first wakes up? Precisely, *fear* wakes up because it rings a bell TING ... in the brain. Other emotions watch the cinema.

In present every day we read articles, listen to the news, and financial crises, inflation, price increases, deflation, depression in the economy, threats to petrol supply, the disaster of currency, hazards in capitalism, the collapse of the economy, insolvent banks, the jeopardy in the property market, labourer strike and suicide by businessman, etc. It challenges philosophies and looks forward to the best solutions.

I am not looking at Das Capital and Capital from a statistical point of view; I look at it from life. It is my synthesis.

The Communist Manifesto was the manifesto of the spectre, and Das Capital is the manifesto of the vampire. We can see the whole picture when we put them on Canon. We can hear the song of the spectre and see the dance of vampire. In human history, we are listening to the wonderful music of the transformation first time. It is fascinating music. I fearmorphosised 19th century *Das Capital*, 20th-century *Metamorphosis*, *The Myth of Sisyphus*, and *No Exit* together in the 21st century in the form of scientific, space, planet, satellite, and the cyber universe. In time intervals, the meaning of capital might change but the heart remains constant. What the fear, pain, and suffering were in England in the 19th century during the industrial revolution, similar revolutions exist in many countries at present. So, capital, labor power, wage, surplus value, surplus profit, overtime work, labor act, labour law, interest, loan, rent, and capital law must show present in the past myths, scapegoats, and Panopticons. Several countries' workers' housing, food, cloth, schooling, health, and life is worsened today than in the 1815-1900 century of Europe. Thus, fearmorphosis shows the movie of the past in 4DX theatre.

One of the very popular concepts of Marx is *alienation*. Sisyphus was alien, he rolled up and down a boulder. Gregor Samsa was alien. He was suffocated in the insect room. The capitalist and labourer are alien Sisyphus. Who is alien according to Karl Marx? The proletarian Sisyphus is alien. Under fearism surveillances, everyone is an alien Sisyphus.

Capital, money, investment, asset, property, and stock are stones. A Sisyphus rams it up and up. From the summit, it falls down. He never leaves his hope. He does it again and again. He repeats it until he lives. Man is prior to capital. He is a rock; he heaves up himself and his stone.

Life, society, capital, and politics are in a fearmorphosis. We have Sisyphus, Panopticon, scapegoat, and Bhageeratha concepts. Between Panopticon and Sisyphus which is young and which is old, is still unclear. Somehow both have flesh and blood relation. They are walking and working side by side since first consciousness evolved. Their parental role structured society and developed. We are under their canopy.

The seed of Das Capital was in the Communist Manifesto. Plantation season was not good in 1848 and left implantation there. In 1867 it was the best season for the plantation, it was planted. It grew into an unhealthy plant, later became healthy, and was spread all over the world in the name of communism.

K. C. Sunbeam writes, it certainly includes infusing Mr. Subba's "fear factor," which I prefer to call original and innate self-preservation impulses, which Marxism fails to adequately address. Specifically, he wants to change Marxism's dialectic materialism into "fearological materialism." Desh also declares that Marx "turned upside down on its head much of Hegel" (guiding principles of the great 18th-19th century philosopher Georg Hegel). Also, being a philosopher, Mr. Subba would have been especially impacted by prevailing Marxist ideology. Hence why he continues to mentally wrestle with it. This wrestling continues for most of the book. However, don't even entertain the notion that Desh considers political solutions as any universal panacea [1].

Some references we can read from the Communist Manifesto:

A spectre is haunting Europe—the spectre of communism [2].

Communist Manifesto is a mother of Das Capital. It was born, grew, and spread all over the world. The baby spectre of Manifesto became an earthly vampire and Eleos. At present, its several variants can be seen. The baby was for basic needs; it grew in the name of means of subsistence. Means of subsistence are socialized and popularized throughout the book.

The history of all hitherto existing societies is the history of class struggle [3].

Karl Marx's quote cannot satisfy my philosophical desire. So, I rejected it. My logic is, in the beginning, a man was single and later became a couple. They were the starter of society. The mythical and religious texts proved it. Where is the class here? They had many crises. When we walk in a lonely place, in dark, we fear. When, 2, 3...10 people walk side by side, we become fearless. So, my argument is the history of all hitherto existing societies is the history of fear struggle.

In proportion to the bourgeoisie, i.e., capital is developed, in the same proportion is the proletariat, the modern working class, a developed class of labourers, who live only so long as they find work, and who find work only so long as their labour increases capital. These labourers, who must sell themselves piecemeal, are a commodity, like every other article of commerce, and are consequently exposed to all the vicissitudes of competition, to all the fluctuations of the market [4].

Major descriptions of Das Capital are enveloped. A proletariat was fear Sisyphus; he sold his commodity. His commodity is equivalent to the article of commerce. He was in a fear struggle. Why did he metamorphose into a man, a commodity, a commercial article, and a Sisyphus? Do we see any class struggle in the metamorphosis of a frog? Every living thing is changing to secure life as previously said by Krishna Dharabasi. Das Capital is the transformation of the communist manifesto. According to season (time), and location (space) it metamorphoses.

The proletariat goes through various stages of development. With its birth begins its struggle with the bourgeoisie. At first, the contest is carried on by individual labourers, then by the working people of a factory, then by the operatives of one trade, in one locality, against the individual bourgeois who directly exploits them [5].

The proletariat goes through various stages of conversion. In every stage, he struggles. The birth begins from the amygdala. Self (himself), Internal (individual labourers), and externals (factory workers, traders, locality, and bourgeois) are the footsteps to the summit. These steps are Marxist ways. It has Kanchenjunga, Karakoram, and more mountains to reach Sagarmatha.

At this stage, therefore, the proletarians do not fight their enemies, but the enemies of their enemies, the remnants of absolute monarchy, the landowners, the non-industrial bourgeoisie, the bourgeoisie [6].

In the beginning, Marx said the history of class struggle, but he accepted many other wrestles. He uses synonyms of struggle like a contest, competition, and fight. The forms of enemies were internal and external. At the struggle, always comes afraid.

Wages labour rests exclusively on competition between the labours [7].

It strongly contradicts the Marxist basic assumption. Sartre contradicted between Existence precedes Essence and Hell is other people. Wages labour compete with wages labour, and capitalists compete with the capitalist. Marx accepted that battles always happened among the hostile brothers but writes about class struggle. He contradicts himself.

From the moment when labour can no longer be converted into capital, money, or rent, into a social power capable of being monopolized, i.e., from the moment when individual property can no longer be transformed into bourgeois property, into capital, from that moment, you say, individuality vanishes [8].

A labourer converts into a commodity. That commodity is saleable. Nobody buys old-age labourers because they cannot push carts. A direct example of it is a slave. One employee hires by a company and hand-to-hand sales to many companies. The company makes money through them. Such several companies are doing business at present.

Camus contradict Marxism, the Marxists, and their followers likewise thinking they are humanists. But for them, human nature will be formed in the classless society of the future. They reject the man of today in the name of the man of the future. That claim is religious in nature [9].

More or less I am convinced by Camus's accusation. It is the cause I forwarded to fearmorphosis. Such change was never recorded in the past, and will not happen again in the future. And, Marx has taken the same step of the dance only the footsteps differ. He wrote, "The miserable routine of endless drudgery and toil in which the same mechanical process is gone through over and over again, is like the labour of Sisyphus. The burden of labour, like the rock, keeps ever falling back on the worn-out labourer [10].

Marx has written first about labourer Sisyphus. Camus wrote proletariat Sisyphus. Camus and Marx both have a single mechanical pushing a rock. They never thought of the spiritual Panopticon and labour scapegoat. Was the work of Sisyphus not being watched by Panopticons? Theophobia was the reason for his miserable routine of endless drudgery and toil. Life of the people is not like Sisyphus's all the time and the same mechanical process is not gone through over and over again. We are option explorers. We work on the basis of the best option.

Camus talked about proletarian Sisyphus in the myth of Sisyphus. He writes, Sisyphus, proletarian of the gods, powerless and rebellious, knows the whole extent of his wretched condition: it is what he thinks of during his descent [11].

Every thinker has the pronoun and synonym of Sisyphus. They apply them accordingly. He has written as powerless. Mostly powerless can be scapegoated for any reason. Zeus and Æsopus scapegoated him because he was powerless in comparison to them.

Das Capital is a sketch of the story. In the story, he has shown life, work, working place, labor, laborer, profit, capital, interest, exploitation, rules, news, laws, statements of a Bank manager, trade, shipping, cotton, textile, the living condition of the laborer, rent of land since 1844 to 1870. Sometimes some dates go beyond.

The life of man is very fragile at any moment it can break. It doesn't need a big reason. Simply hold the neck and stop breathing, and it ends. It can be applied in philosophy as well. Soren Kierkegaard, Fyodor Dostoevsky, and Friedrich Nietzsche were existentialist philosophers. Their whole idea is superseded by Jean-Paul Sartre who said, "Existence precedes essence". Kafka, Sartre, and Camus's work is collectively fearmorphoses in this text. In Das Capital whatever is said in a massive dissertation (1392 pages), its foundation is the means of subsistence. It is played like stereotypes a hundred times. Anonymously it is written. Means of subsistence links to survival and it internets to fear. Many synonyms of fear are applied in the book. *No Exit* was written to show 'Hell is other people' but a number of fear and its sisters are unknowingly written therein.

Karl Marx lived for 33 years in London (1849-1883). The story of Das Capital is his first-hand book. He visited most of the places that are mentioned in the story. What he saw, what he felt, poverty, poor condition of housing, and bad health conditions of workers, he has recorded.

Liberty means freedom from fear and fear-self. The concept of God's death and the author's death changed the world's prior concept. End of the Marxism has a similar sense. It is a changing idea. Marxism is in front of us, a great wall (God, author). It closed the panorama views of the world. The curtain must be lifted up. It is a ruler, which ruled for 200 years and is still ruling in some countries.

In history no one rules forever. No matter how pervasive it is, one day, it must collapse. Once it terminates, it opens a new Everest from there can view a panorama of the Himalayas, sea, and forest. In the Allegory of Cave, when a philosopher existed, he saw the real world which was shadowed by hallucination.

To sustain philosophy, one word, or sentence is enough. The main point is how the philosopher has presented it. Put on canon, its logic, reference, and argument. Marxism stands on the matter; class is its breath. If it is eliminated it naturally ends. Fearism can be ended if people live in absence of the amygdala, but without the amygdala, generally, no one exists. Kasper Renee Johansen writes, "For fearism, fear is embedded in our biology. Like the amygdala, also popularly called the fear center of the brain, fear is present everywhere in the animal kingdom" [12].

Capitalism is the binary opposition to Marxism. The hand, mind, sense, and leg are all human organs; are functional as a man is breathing. When the breath stops, all parts die. Marxism's utopia is communism, but society is interneting in the cyber world.

Low wages, and surplus work, have given wide space in the fable, but why manv must effort, is not mentioned. In the slave era, slaves were compelled to work, in the Industrial Revolution, workers were not constrained by capitalists. They desired themselves. Why did they desire it? Were they forced on by the bourgeois? No, then what was the force?

Marx argues, as cliches, about low wages, and exploitation by the capitalist. If workers didn't want to work, capitalists had to pay high wages, and in crisis, inevitably compel them.

When they offered low wages, then they had sole authority to negate. Starvation, infernal life, illiteracy, unhealthy, and prestige was reason to work at a low wage. People's fright compels them to duty at any cost. The capitalists were not exploiters of labor; the original suckers were fears. If they didn't have it, capitalists had no chance to exploit them.

Was originally a man a labourer? By birth was he a Sisyphus? Why did a man convert into Sisyphus? Why did Camus write manv effort? Why had he put himself in the market? Did he know the form of his Bhageeratha labor? Was it inevitable to display him in the market? Did he do it himself or by the capitalist?

What are the differences between the classical form and the present form of employees? Were capitalists not selling them in the form of finance? Can we read all these in the hierarchy of commodities? What is the common factor? These come under Sotalism. It is the 201st-century hybrid form of the economic system—that is, Capitalism + Socialism [13].

Look! How scary a face we have today. Does it begin from profit or expenditure? From the hunting age to Sotalism, subsistence is contained. Labor-power, surplus value, profit, and capitalism depend on it. It is a yolk protected by albumen and shell as a theory of egg mentioned in Trans Philosophism [14].

Let's view the earth, a new world can be seen from the fearmorphosis. It is open. We need to see the world from this tower.

A. Legend of Bhageeratha

Bhageeratha was a king of Kosala, a kingdom of ancient India. He was a descendent of the great king Sagara of the Suryavamsa, or Sun Dynasty. When king Sagara chose to perform the Ashwamedha yagna, his royal agents lost track of the sacrificial horse. Sagara ordered his sixty thousand sons by Sumati to track down the horse. The proud and mercurial princes raged across Bharat, burning down forests and uprooting life and property to find the horse.

They finally arrived at a quiet spot where the Sage Kapila was sitting in meditation. Besides him was tied the white horse. The enraged princes condemned Kapila as a thief and attacked him. Using his terrible mystic power, Kapila instantly turned the princes into ashes. One version has it that Kapila told the prince Anshuman, Sagara's grandson (Son of Asamanjan, other son of Sagara who was thrown out of kingdom by him) who had come looking both for the horse and his brothers, that the only way for the souls of the dead princes could rise to heaven would be through the offering of niravapanjali with the water of the sacred Ganga river, which was flowing only in Swarga.

Bringing Ganga back to Earth was a near impossible task and required many years to be spent in tapasya and prayer. The Kosala kings of successive generations could not do this while managing their duties as kings. As a result, the sins of the thousand princes multiplied in their destructive energy, and began resulting in natural disasters. The kingdom began to lose its peace and prosperity, and by the time Bhageeratha ascended the throne, he found it impossible to attempt to govern in this situation, that had only one solution.

Turning over the kingdom to trusted ministers, Bhageeratha set off to the Himalayas to perform an arduous tapasya in the extreme climate. For one thousand years, he performed an excruciatingly harsh penance to please Lord Brahma. At the end of the thousand years, Brahma came to him and told him to ask for anything. Bhageeratha asked Brahma to bring down the river Ganga to earth so that he may perform the ceremony for his ancestors.

Brahma asked Bhageeratha to propitiate Lord Shiva, for only He would be able to break the Ganga's fall. It was the largest river, and it would be impossible for anyone save Him to contain the destructive impact of this event.

Bhageeratha performed a tapasya for Lord Shiva, living only on air. The compassionate Shiva appeared only after a year's penance and told Bhageeratha he should not have to perform tapasya to accomplish a noble goal such as this. He assured Bhageeratha that he would break Ganga's fall.

After eons of being flattered and praised by the Devas, Ganga had become vain. She scoffed at Brahma when He asked her to flow down to earth but could not disobey him as he was her father.

But Ganga was sure, as much as Bhageeratha was afraid that no one could stop her fall, which would devastate the earth for a long time. As she cascaded across and down from Swarga, Bhageeratha and celestial observers were terrified of the roar and volume of water coming down. But Lord Shiva appeared from out of nowhere and captured all of Ganga just as she launched herself onto earth, in His jata.

Ganga struggled to set herself free, but Shiva could not be budged. Bhageeratha worshipped Shiva, who let Ganga free after crushing her vanity. She flowed, and is still believed to flow, from Shiva's jata down to earth at a gentler pace.

King Bhageeratha led the way for Ganga on his chariot, and she followed him across the north and east of Bharat and finally merging with the ocean. In her course she washed the ashes of Sagara's sixty thousand sons, who ascended to heaven while praising and blessing Bhageeratha. Bhageeratha's own great effort was praised by all the Gods and his ancestors, and is known as a Bhageeratha Prayatna, as proclaimed by Lord Brahma. It is a great inspiration to any man who seeks to do something noble despite facing overwhelming odds [15].

Bhageeratha labour is very important in human life. His life is a paradigm for any labor dedicated person. It can be applicable to workers, businessmen, sportsmen, politicians, thinkers, philosophers, and authors. I use Bhageeratha Prayatna for instance of a successful career. Success can be achieved through hard Pryatna. Bhageeratha pryatna gives a message of hard work until one reaches to the peak. It is a popular legend in the East.

Capital Man

A man debuted in the capital. It is the first capital. Its lucid example is a slave. Slaves were commodities. They could sell, buy, deposit, rent, transfer, and exchange. A man looked at the external like musk deer. Male Musk deer have a gland that produces musk, an important ingredient in perfumery. We have a proverb in Nepal, it smells of fragrance in the forest; try to find from where the aroma sprays. Musk doesn't know it comes from the body.

In the forest many animals live. They have a radical nature. Among them, there are several species of tigers. They have various behaviours, silent moving and looking around their surroundings are common. The prey often alerts to escape.

To find means of subsistence, a man followed the tiger's steps. As Lenin analyzed, the developed form of capitalism is imperialism. They took tiger steps to colonized weaker countries. SSS is not far from tiger steps because they psychologically and mentally hunt them. Karl Marx predicted capitalists exploit proletariats; eventually, they revolt. As his prediction, none of the countries revolted. Instead of it, laborers were happy, their living standard was upgraded. It shocked him and it made him sad and depressed. The solution was given by Lenin after a long time of his death in the book, *Imperialism, the Highest Stage of Capitalism was Imperialism* (1917). According to him, imperialists exploited colonies and a nominal portion of the income they allocated to workers. Though they were exploited their living standard was improved. In this condition, they did not revolt.

The credit for capitalism goes to Liberalism, Utilitarianism, and the economic theory of Adam Smith. They focused non-interference of the government in business and industry. They promoted private property and the birth of capitalism. Karl Marx criticized the free-market policy. He was supportive of communism. The industrial revolutions gave him fertile soil to grow historical materialism.

In many factories, labourers were working at the time when Marx entered England. The assumption, they worked eight hours a day—it was normal condition. It demands normal relations to the environment, politics, and economy. This system ran the economy, life, society, etc. If one screw cracks then the whole system might crack down. It depended on the size of the accident. A big accident badly affected the system.

Marx observed the proletariat Sisyphus. He became Sisyphus by his fear. Not only he, the myth of Sisyphus, proletarian, capitalist, and any professional becomes Sisyphus by their fear. Karl Marx was Sisyphus of materialism. He heaved up it till his death.

A boy came and told, "I am hungry for several days, please give me a job, I work without a wage." In this condition, can it be consider exploitation? No, because a boy sells his Bhageeratha for food. It is happening in many countries. Millions of people are struggling for food. It has two conditions if a capitalist forcefully uses labour power, it is exploitation; if a boy voluntarily offers, it is not exploitation. The capitalists develop a super fear structure, it is the question of concern here.

Labour power doesn't operate itself and it doesn't operate in the same ratio all the time. Does Sisyphus operate himself? At barbarian phase, what operated to motivate a man to hunt? It was hunger. The size of hunger decides labour-power. Its subordinates were environment, family, society, health, beliefs, and position. Once, labour-power varies, it changes working hours, Acts, surplus-value, market, production, profit, etc. Labour-power depends on suffering, tragedy, pain, crisis, trouble, and problems.

Was Gregor Samsa willing to be a salesboy? We cannot see it in *Metamorphosis*.

Since, primitive times, we are preserving it and carrying together with civilization. Several Acts have been made like 1833, 1844, 1847, 1850, 1863, and so on are mentioned in the book. It came to protect life from the over-working of children, young, adult, and the aged. The worker knew he had been exploited but could not revolt. Machines took away almost all jobs. Day by day the standard of workers was degraded.

The story is the Marxist's eye on the capital system. The commodity is that object, which plays a significant role in our subsistence. We have two types of commodities: 1. One is for subsistence, 2. Other is for facilitating our life. We are not enumerating natural objects. When it becomes a commodity, we calculate it in economic terms. Both come from raw material ends in the finished product. These processes need Bhageeratha. Now, it became three; raw material, Bhageeratha, and finished product. In manufacturing wage, profit, finance, loss, economy, capital, insurance, cargo, storage, shipping, exploitation, labor, capitalist, corruption, loan, credit, rent, interest, and bankruptcy, appears. Das Capital is the master of it. Everything comes in the periphery of commodity, money, and labour (C-M-L).

We filter our goals before selecting the best in life. Likewise, I filtered Das Capital and took fearmaterials for the purpose of this book. The story of Das Capital is a gross idea, incomplete, and somewhat distortive, from a fearism speculation and lens.

Thoughts on Conditions:

1st I want to sell my labour-power. The question comes, why do I want to sell?

2nd Please sell me your labour-power. Why does he want to buy it?

3rd You must buy it. Why do I threaten him?

4th You must sell me. Why does he warn me to sell?

These are the conditions that makes difference in the labour market. It applies to manufacturers, buyers, and sellers.

Above, we see the conditions of helpless, poor, and panic workers. If I couldn't sell my Bhageeratha, my family suffers from various problems. After Gregor transformed into vermin, still he was worried about family maintenance. A gap between the *Sudama and the *Kubera came from the motion of society. In society, some became

Kubera, and some became Sudama. Those who did manv effort used skills and did innovative work, and became rich. Neither it is by capitalism nor by fate. Even today, people are working 18 hours in some countries, sometimes 24 hours (at home and office), because their income is not enough to bear market prices and appetite desire.

Normally, capitalists work more hours than workers but it is unnoticed. The capitalist has money, the worker has a stomach appetite.

Both Sisyphuses, capitalist and worker form, are separate in nature. During the Industrial Revolution, people had less expense and less competition in comparison to the present world. At present they must pay, rent, water, electricity, education, a mortgage on a vehicle, house, appliances, government duties, dress, food, internet, health care, cosmetics, and telephone bills, etc. Consequently, people metamorphose into Gregor Sisyphus and push rocks for additional hours. Are they doing it themselves?

A similar case was in the 18th to 19th centuries in Europe. So, I concluded that it was not exploitation. Were Sisyphus and Bhageeratha exploited? In voluntary work and in punishment, there is no exploitation. It was a survival crisis. In a crisis, everyone metamorphoses into cunning Sisyphus.

When we observe the exploitation scenario, developed countries are exploiting poor and developing countries. I call it, Net Exploitation because there is nothing gross. The exploitation of industry or capitalism is gross because it is a mixed labor-power, family, and social crisis. The sale of Bhageeratha is a compulsion of labourers, but exploitation by colonists had no compulsion. Colonizers did not exploit only for surplus-value; they exploited the blood, flesh, and breath of people. They colonized, scapegoated, and sold in the market.

In the story, nothing is mentioned about a civil servant and the army. In a society, labor, capitalist, employed, and self-employed people reside. Self-employed occupations were ignored and misunderstood.

The question comes to our mind, why do we need human commodities? Does it come to make money? In Marxism's eye, these were diamonds. Is it the right answer? What was their use? Have we asked ourselves? Commodity exchanges to money. What relation has between commodity and money with capital? These questions were unanswered. We are followers. My effort is to find the actual story of Das Capital. To have the best life, we look at multiple options. My dissertation is the synthesis.

*Sudama= He is a friend of Krishna. He represents a poor man.

*Kubera=He is a god of wealth. He represents a wealthy man.

Human Capital

The Hunting Age was a seed and bud of capital. At this age, humans laboured to hunt an animal. The hunted animal was their property. It belonged to them. During this period, they invented weapons. Tools were manufactured to manage the means of production. Means of subsistence was the primary task of a man. The hunting folk manufactured, produced, and distributed it. It could only be accomplished by brave and rational folks of that time.

Whoever invented a stone weapon, was his asset. Likewise, who killed an animal for food, was his property. Another person, borrowed, exchanged with labour-power, goods, and something else that which inventor required. The prey he killed, he shared with others because everyone couldn't get meat. The starvation conditions desired food. He gave them. But, in exchange, he wanted something from takers. He became a commander of food and he had its power *via* his right. When it was a hand-to-hand transfer, it became a commodity. It was also applicable to fruit, vegetable, and roots.

In all seasons, fruit, vegetable, and roots were not available. First, who stored them effectively, he became Hero in a group. A person who had food survived longer; who had little or none was more vulnerable, and could perish before time. Still, we can view this relation in the indigenous communities. Suppose a man kills a pig. The villagers or community members gather and share it. Some take in credit, some labour costs, and some exchange with other things. They are the representative of our ancestors. Even, at present, if a man kills a boar, they follow the same merchandise. It was the foundation of capitalism and the economic system.

According to Yuval Noah Harrari, the last common grandmother of humans and chimpanzees was started six million years ago. In Africa, 2.5 million years ago the genus *Homo* evolved, the first stone tools crafted substantially. And 12,000 years ago agricultural and animal domestication was taking place. Between the stone tool and the domestication of plants, there is a long gap. I am not agreeing that land was the first private property as said by Locke and some other social contract thinkers. Life, prey, and the stone tool was the first commodity and private property. The hunting profession was older than farming. From these travelled the manufacture, production, factory, industry, merchandise, finance, bank, rent, loan, labour, profit, loss, insurance, and currency. The trade started with stone weapons, but professional trade began with the occupation of land.

A commodity is, in the first place, an object outside us, a thing that by its properties satisfies human wants of some sort or another [16].

We are the first commodity. We need to examine human emotion and want. The commodities were not started in the Industrial Revolution; it was started long ago. In the historical record, the alarm (fear) was prior to wanting. It is not a question of satisfying human wants, it was of securing life. After secure life, then, comes desire and want. Such is the view of the fearist perspective, in my view.

As William Petty puts it, labour is its father and the earth is its mother [17]. William Petty has given beautiful words like Purush and Prakirti. In other terms, labour is Purush and Prakirti is the land. Its combination creates the commodity, and means of subsistence. We exist in the world because of our parents. While the land was unused, they lived by hunting.

The form of wood, for instance, is altered, by making a table out of it. Yet, for all that, the table continues to be that common, every-day thing, wood. But, as soon as it steps forth as a commodity, it is changed into something transcendent. It not only stands with its feet on the ground, but, in relation to all other commodities, it stands in its head, and evolves out of its wooden brain grosteque ideas, far more wonderful than "table-turning" ever was [18].

The wood is valueless until mixed with labour. Why does a man mix labour? Because he must have food for basic needs.

Marx uses, want but want, and basic need is different. Basic need is for subsistence; want is for extravagant. Wood becomes table after adding labour.

Why does it need to add labour? It has two reasons, 1. Add the value of labour, 2. A labourer does labour for his and his family's maintenance. Labour gives the commodity value of wood. Now, the commodity has market value; added value is labour. So, he claims his price. With the price, he buys his basic needs.

Could commodities themselves speak, they would say; 'Our use value may be a thing that interests men' [19]. The commodities never speak. Firstly, labour and capitalist speak. Secondly, story speaks on behalf of the commodity. Does Marxism voice represent a commodity? What do the commodities want to speak about?

Does Sisyphus speak? The rock and Sisyphus don't speak, myth teller speaks. A stone, commodity, labour cannot explain by word and language. The meaning of society, the commodity is not as explained by Marx, and neither it is as said by me. The real value of a commodity is noumena in Kant's language. He said, the thing itself. Word and language are signifiers of the object. They speak because commodities keep silent. Commodities and Subaltern issues are dissimilar. Subalterns are human beings, according to Aristotle, they can use logos, some postmodernists say, the subaltern cannot speak. Commodities speak through the mouth of a man. That is a phenomenon.

Now listen to how those commodities speak through the mouth of the economist [20]. The commodity speaks through the mouth of the labour, capitalist, economist, philosopher, and fearist. Das Capital, speaks through Karl Marx. Now fearmorphosis speaks in my voice. What does it link to it? Does it link to the economy, Marxism, or subsistence? Fearism argues it links to means of subsistence. Eventually, it speaks the stomach.

Money Market

In history, it is difficult to trace the origin of money. However, it was invented to facilitate human life. In the presence of it, our life became more convenient. If we remove it from use, it will be hard to do any transactions?

People have different opinions regarding the genesis of money. Wikipedia notes, from about 1000 BC, money in the form of small knives and spades made of bronze was in use in China during the Zhou dynasty, with cast bronze replicas of cowrie shells in use before this. The first manufactured actual coins seem to have appeared separately in India, China, and the cities around the Aegean Sea 7th century BC.

While these Aegean coins were stamped (heated and hammered with insignia), the Indian coins (from the Ganges river valley) were punched metal disks, and Chinese coins (first developed in the Great Plain) were cast bronze with holes in the center to be strung together. The different forms and metallurgical processes imply a separate development [21].

Karl Marx writes of nomadic races which were the first to develop the money form. It was because all their worldly goods consist of moveable objects and are therefore directly alienable; and because of their mode of life, by continually bringing them into contact with foreign communities, they solicit the exchange of products [22]. He suggests basic needs-commodity-barter system-money were evolutionary as part of money. First, the crisis of survival needs came, and after that commodity, barter system, money, and the bank respectively. If the life threat appears, it reverses again. Nomadic races as they developed were not activated themselves beyond basic exchange. Only after a long time of development, it transformed into capital.

The increment of the excess over the original value I call "surplus-value" [23], Marx wrote. Meaning of surplus-value was given by Karl Marx. According to him, the increment of the excess over the original value is surplus-value. Why do we need surplus-value is the question? The original value depends upon the situation. The commodity is very useful and rare, its original value remains high. When it is decorated and crafted its value increase. If that commodity is handled by a skilled craftsman increases its value. If the craftsman is not skilled, then the value decrease. Sometimes, damage too. Surplus value is added to the original value. It begins with raw materials and finishes with the product value. Sometimes one finished product becomes raw material for another product. The Myth of Sisyphus and Das Capital became the raw material for fearmorphosis. Every raw material needs to add labour to take the next finished product. Fearmorphosis is the raw material for another finished product.

The boundless greed after riches, this passionate chase after exchange-value is common to the capitalist and the miser; but while the miser is merely a capitalist gone mad, the capitalist is a rational miser [24].

Why do capitalists have boundless greed after rich? It is similar to Sisyphus when he had seen the face of this world, enjoyed water and sun, warm stones, and the sea, he no longer wanted to go back to the infernal darkness [25]. The capitalist also didn't want to go back to the inferno. Merely were they greedy, not others? Everyone was fascinated by greed, but the degree was varying. Their final cause was happiness. Was the capitalist a rational miser? The capitalist was more Bhageeratha than a rational miser. He rolled his capital as much as to the topmost because hell was behind him.

Thus in the oldest caves, we find stone implements and weapons. In the earliest period of human history domesticated animals, i.e., animals which have been bred for the purpose, and have undergone modifications by means of labour, play the chief part as instruments of labour along with specially prepared stones, wood, bones, and shells. The use and fabrication of instruments of labour, although existing in the germ among certain species of animals, is especially characteristic of human labour-process, and Franklin therefore defines man as a tool-making animal [26].

Weapons were not produced for business; rather, were built to lessen the fear and rescue life. Stone, wood, bone, and shell were materials to build weapons. Tools helped them and preserved life; functioned as armor. And 12,000 years before the dog was the first domesticated animal, main duty of a dog was to protect the master.

The definition of Franklin denotes man as a tool-making animal, but why was he a tool-making animal? Now, the weapon became the largest business in the world. How largest is not important, its ultimate object is to reduce fear as in the hunting society. Weapons and economy are part of fear management basics.

The general character of the labour-process is evidently not changed by the fact, that the labourer works for the capitalist instead of for himself [27].

It is absurd as Camus's Sisyphus. Did Bhageeratha labour for Lord Shiva? Labourer works for himself and his family's maintenance. Did Samsa work for an employer? Nobody intimidates him to work. His catastrophe obliges him. Nowadays several of them are self-employed, are they working for the capitalist? No, they are working for themselves.

Every day brings a man 24 hours nearer to his grave: but how many days he can still to travel on that road, no man can tell accurately by merely looking at him [28].

Marx thought labourer's life is closer to the grave. He guessed their life is in danger and at any time can go to the cemetery. How many days he travelled the steep mountain, nobody tells. How many days did Sisyphus heave up his boulder, Homer, Odyssey, Iliad, and Camus didn't know? Bhageeratha didn't know when Ganga comes down to the earth. Terror of life was a question. It is applicable to everyone because the grave is for all.

One day, we have to rest in peace. It doesn't bias workers or capitalists. A peaceful, silent, and last destination of manv's place is a grave. We can imagine how fragile is our life.

A violent interruption of the labour-process by a crisis, makes him sensitively aware of it [29].

The crisis is the chief factor to sell labour. In the selling, any kind of violence may be interrupted, so, he must be aware. This is a sort of alarm, it TONG ..bells him all the time. The capitalist is not excluded, another Conch tunes to him.

The rate of surplus-value is therefore an exact expression for the degree of exploitation of labour-power by capital, or of the labourer by the capitalist [30].

It can be accepted on one condition but why does a labourer accept surplus hours? Gregor worked for five years without taking a holiday. A man has an endless desire, as an endless mountain-top, to reach there, he needs surplus money. If he rejects can capitalists compel him? At present, the capitalist doesn't have that authority. Suppose Sisyphus is born today, he doesn't roll his stone. Yes, termination is possible. He rolls his employment of fear to the topmost.

Vampire Capital

Karl Marx and Friedrich Engels use vampire and spectre. The Communist Manifesto is the manifesto of the spectre because the spectre is the hero of part one. The Communist Manifesto is part one and Das Capital is part two. The movie begins with it and plays all around it.

Their accusation was the capitalist's fear of the rising communist spectre. So, they made an alliance. It was a preposterous accusation. On the contrary, the communist made unions, associations, committees, etc. The proletariats were afraid of the bourgeois, thus they raised the revolutionary slogan, "workingmen, unite." However, vampire, spectre, ghost, witch, and Dracula are characters in parts 1 and 2. In the story, ghost's suck and wash humans' brain. The authors' image was, capitalists suck the blood of the proletariat. What was the reality; the first part we have seen above, and the second part we see below.

Capital is dead labour, that vampire-like only lives by sucking living labour, and lives the more, the more labour it sucks [31].

Marx alleged, a capitalist sucks labour like a vampire. A vampire quenches the blood of a living man and converting to a living capital. It sucks the sweat and blood of the proletariat.

As said above, the capitalist's role is a vampire or Santa (Claus), depending on the situation. Some believe in Santa and some believe in vampire.

Children of nine or ten years are dragged from their squalid beds at two, three or four o'clock in the morning and compelled to work for a bare subsistence until ten, eleven, or twelve at night, their limbs wearing away, their frames dwindling their faces whitening, and their humanity absolutely sinking into a stone-like torpor, utterly horrible to contemplate [32].

This picture shows the 19th century Western World; a terrible and high level of cruelty. It is a real sense of exploitation. Children were not at the age to work, and they were not willing. In this context, the character of a capitalist was a vampire. Why they became Dracula(?); because they were afraid of losing income. They could make more money as much as they became pitiless. Cruelty was Zeus in the Iliad. Zeus kidnapped Ægina, here the vampire sips the blood of underage children.

In the last week of June 1863, all the London daily papers published a paragraph with the "sensational" heading, "Death from simple over-work, "It deals with the death of the milliner, Mary Anne Walkley, 20 years of age, employed in highly respectable dressmaking establishment, exploited by a lady with the pleasant name of Elise [33].

In this sensational news, a lady Mary Anne Walkley employed in Elise's dressmaking business. The employer ordered her to do overwork. It might be the cause of her death. Elise was accused of it. She was secondary. The primary cause was her subsistence crisis.

Every day many people died from starvation, unhealthy water, and worse living. The death rate of such cases is more at present. Particularly, it happens more in cities than in villages. The village has fresh air and less burden.

The urban public has more boulders and dark skies. So, the death of Mary was the cause of the mental boulder. Heidegger argues, "The only reality is "anxiety" in the whole chain of begins. To the man lost in the world and its diversions, this anxiety is a brief, fleeing fear. But if that fear becomes conscious of itself, it becomes anguish the perpetual climate of the lucid man "in whom existence is concentrated" [34].

In order to give the doctor a lesson in good manners, the coroner's jury thereupon brought in a verdict that "the deceased had died of apoplexy, but there saw reason to fear that her death had been accelerated by over-work in an over-crowded workroom, etc." [35].

In order to give the doctor a lesson in a good manner, the coroner's jury thereupon brought in a verdict, the jury wanted a good working environment for workers, it is written: "The deceased (Mary Anne Walkley) had died of apoplexy, but the cause of death was fear that she had been accelerated by over-work in an over-crowded workroom, etc." Fear was the boulder that crushed her life. It was covered in the doctor's report.

Nonye T Aghanya writes, I began to study the work of various philosophers and their own interpretation of Fear. I recently read R. Michael Fisher's 2015 publication "Educating Ourselves: A Lovist or Fearist Perspective." I was fascinated by his introductory paragraph that detailed as a fearist, his observation of a correlation between how we live our lives and how we educate ourselves [36].

It quenches only to a slight degree the vampire's thirst for the living blood of labour [37].

The prolongation of the working day beyond the limits of the natural day, into the night. Marx indicated that vampires quench the thirst from the blood of labourer. Working 10, 12, and 16 hours a day was only a part degree for them. They wanted 24 hours. Marx wanted to show capitalists' blood-shedding fierce teeth.

Giant vampires like China and India are emerging. Its effects can be seen in the capital world.

B. Means of Subsistence

Mode of Living

Every man has his own draft of living. He sketches and draws a picture. His destination depends on the environment. The road might be difficult, steep, slope, hilly, muddy, desert, swampy, or zigzag; and, he has to drive accordingly.

Any wrong drive happens in an accident. At the time of the steam engine, a challenging life was ahead. It was steep slope for coolies. However, they had to carry luggage. The steam engine was a boulder on the way. It devoured their livelihood. The living was in danger. They had to move upward carefully.

The fearful increase in death from starvation during the last 10 years in London runs parallel with the extension of sewing machine [38].

Why did Marx use the fearful increase in death from starvation during the last 10 years in London? Because the situation was scary.

And, it was by extension, a sewing machine responsible for the deaths from starvation? Suppose we agree with him, at present millions of machines are in use. Why has rate of dying from starvation not increased?

So, machines were not condemned to those miserable conditions. The best fear government could manage the situation but it was lacking. The weakness and carelessness of governments scapegoated them. It was not due to the extension of the sewing machine. Only a philosopher-ruler is the best to rule a nation as said by Plato, but the best ruler ought to be a fearism philosopher.

We have seen how this absolute contradiction between the technical necessities of modern industries, and the social character inherent in its capitalist form, dispels all fixity and security in the situation of the labourer, how it constantly threatens, by taking away the instruments of labour, to snatch from his hands his means of subsistence and, by suppressing his detailed-function, and, to make him superfluous.

We have seen, too, how this antagonism vents its rage in the creation of that monstrosity, an industrial reserve army, kept in misery to be always at the disposal of capital; in the incessant human sacrifices from among the working class, in the most reckless squandering of labour-power and in the devastation caused by social anarchy which turns every economic progress into a social calamity.

Admittedly, this is the negative side. But if, on the one hand, variation of work at the present imposes itself after the manner of an overpowering natural law, and with the blindly destructive action of a natural law that meets with resistance at all points, modern industry is in question. On the other hand, through its catastrophes it imposes the necessity of recognizing, as a fundamental law of production, variation of work, consequently fitness of labourer for varied work, consequently the greatest possible development of his varied aptitudes.

It becomes a question of life and death for society to adapt the mode of production to the normal functioning of the law. Modern industry, indeed, compels society, under penalty of death, to replace the detail worker of today, grappled by life-long repetition of one and the same trivial operation, and thus reduced to the mere fragment of a man, by the fully developed individual, fit for a variety of labours, ready to face any change of production, and to whom the different social functions he performs, are but so many modes of giving free scope to his own natural and acquired powers [39].

In the incessant human sacrifices from among the working-class, were the form of the scapegoat. Under penalty of death, to replace the worker of today, grappled by life-long repetition of one and the same trivial operation recalls the Sisyphus torture. It outlines continual threats, problems of means of subsistence, antagonism to have it, increases in the number of monstrosities and reserve army, social calamity, catastrophes of modern industry, and penalty of death. The death penalty is strongest than the boulder of Sisyphus but it is rejected by Camus. He said, "There is no more dreadful punishment than futile and hopeless labour."

It was essential to get prosperity as the wish of capitalists. Deaths were behind the rolling stones and capitalists were behind the proletariat Sisyphus. It was a real scene of the story.

Calamities, catastrophes, and the death penalty were imposed on them. To some extent, these forces were applicable to capitalists too. The capitalists heave up their capital to the crest. The infernal darkness even we can see at present. Behind the ram of the boulder, the deadly quarry is the cause. Poor people are living in this hell even today.

When an individual appropriates natural objects for his livelihood, no one controls him but himself [40].

A man is the master and slave himself. Control by Panopticon is absurd. No one can control him except himself. His basic needs control him. In other words, we can say a man is controlled by natural objects and basic needs because it gives breath. He is a major slave of basic needs. It is his God master.

Capital, therefore, it not only, as Adam Smith says, the command over labour. It is essentially the command over unpaid labour [41].

It is a triple play. Marx refutes the capital idea of Adam Smith, I am refuting the Capital concept of Marx. Before going to the command over labour, or unpaid labour, need to see who commands.

It was true that capital commands over labour, but Smith didn't say what commanded over the capital. At the time of fearlessness, the capital could not command them. If money, capital, and power cannot command, then Fear is a commander. Was there capital, and money, in the hunting era? Fear was a military commander. Ancestor *sapiens* were commanded by it.

In previous chapters we saw the destructive consequences of over-work; here we find the sources of the suffering that result to the labourer from his insufficient employment [42].

Yes, the sources of suffering were insufficient employment. It is a reason, I said falling rock is not a happy moment. The sickness of Samsa couldn't be consider a happy moment. To reduce it, coolie must carry overload. When they were overworked, they had more income. Good income reduced their suffering. Bhageeratha brought down Ganga from heaven. In the 21st century, people work more (excessive) hours to meet their dreams.

If the labourer does not possess the average capacity, if he cannot in consequence supply a certain minimum of work per day, he is dismissed [43].

How the Shylock system was imposed on workers. They could be fired if they could not supply a certain capacity of work per day. Somehow, they had to possess the average capacity. At present most companies and employees work day and night. Fear of dismissal they have to push a rock as much as they could as; and on his tip-toes racking all his height; to wrest up to a mountain-top his freight;

Many employees commit suicide and suffer from depression, anxiety, and mental pressure. They must have to meet the customer target otherwise they're dismiss them from the job. It gives high pressure and tension to them.

Fear of discharge, they do Bhageeratha prayatna. The competition is high in the market. They became victims of mental torture. This is the reason, many employees suicide. Camus wanted to show it in his philosophical problem. We can accept, as consequence, it seems, the cause of suicide, depression, anxiety, and mental pressure—is fear.

The exploitation of the labourer by capital is here effected through the exploitation of the labourer by labourer [44].

Sometimes it happened for basic needs and sometimes for a rolling commission. We have rarely heard of that struggle between master and slave but we hear the struggle of Sisyphus vs. Sisyphus and scapegoat vs. scapegoat every day.

Marxist's Shoe

Whatever communists say, whatever we say, whatever somebody says, labourers produce for themselves. When he had abundant production then he bartered and sold to others. Marxists say labour produces for the capitalist; but it is old shoes. A pair of shoes they sewed and wore themselves. They accepted it in many sentences but in the end, played pigeonhole; labour produces for the capitalist.

Somebody asked Socrates "Why do you dislike your wife Xanthippe?" He answered, "My foot knows where it was pinned." Maybe it is applicable to Marx. So, he wrote at times in contradictions. The contradictory statement is in Marxism, which sometimes says, the worker produces for the capitalist, and sometimes says, he produces for himself.

Individual consumption provides, on the one hand, the means for their maintenance and reproduction: on the other hand, it secures by the annihilation of the necessaries of life, the continued re-appearance of the workman in the labour-market.

The Roman slave was held by fetters: the wage-labourer is bound to his owner by invisible threads [45].

Means for their maintenance and reproduction were the priority of the Roman slaves. The Roman slave was held by many fetters. Invisible hands were behind them, as said by Adam Smith. Either Roman slaves or wage labourer, they were scapegoated in the name of their master. Invisible threads are superstructure in Marxism terms. I use SSS and Super Fear Structure (SFS).

He (Mill) quotes the work of a Northamptonshire manufacturer, who, with eyes squinting heaven ward moans; "Labour is one-third cheaper in France than in England; for their work hard, and fare hard, as to their food and clothing. Their cheap diet is bread, fruit, herbs, roots, and dried fish; for they very seldom eat flesh; and when wheat is dear, they eat very little bread" [46].

John Stuart Mill quoted the work of a Northamptonshire manufacturer. At the time of higher wages, labourers ate healthy food and wore better clothing but at the low wages they had the cheapest food, and very seldom ate flesh. The wretch condition of labour was pictured by Mill. It is also applicable to bourgeois and capitalists when they have a good income they enjoy other times cutting off all facilities. At that time England's labour cost was expensive in comparison to France. With such a situation, the farmer is in many countries even today.

He (Gladstone) speaks of masses "on the border" of pauperism, of branches of trade in which" wages have not increased," and finally sums up the happiness of the working class in the words; "human life is but, in nine cases out of ten, a struggle for existence" [47].

Gladstone's Budget speech of April 7th, 1864, was a Pindaric dithyrambus on the advance of surplus-value making and the happiness of the people "tempered by poverty". Not only nine cases out of ten, but all cases were also a struggle for existence in England.

At present, we are struggling for culture, religion, community, language, politics, ecology, and belief. We worry that we will become extinct for any one of many reasons.

Gregor's serious wound, from which he suffered for over a month—since no one ventured to remove the apple, he crept, though he worried about family maintenance.

The insufficiency of food among the agricultural labourers, fell, as a rule, chiefly on the women and children, for "the man must eat to do his work" [48].

The life of the labourer either in agriculture or industry, was difficult. A man couldn't push a rock with an empty stomach. Could Sisyphus heave up his boulder with an empty stomach?

Food was not enough for all. When he ate, his wife and children stayed hungry. Hunger was a killer. Everyone is afraid of demise.

The animal tries the best way to protect life. We are more sensible and conscious than animals. Women and children were scapegoated. If the wife and children were strong, it reversed. The same as if Sisyphus was strong, he punished to Gods.

A frightful spectacle was to be seen yesterday in one part of the metropolis. Although the unemployed thousands of the East-end did not parade with their black flags *en masse*, the human torrent was imposing enough. Let us remember what these people suffer. They were dying of hunger. That is a simple and terrible fact. There are 40,000 of them. In the present, one-quarter of this wonderful metropolis, are packed-next door to the most enormous accumulation of wealth the world ever saw-cheek by jowl with this is 40,000 helpless, starving people.

These thousands are now breaking in upon the quarters; always half-starving, they cry their misery in our ears, they cry to Heaven, and they tell us from their miserable dwellings, that it is impossible for them to find work, and useless for them to beg. The local ratepayers themselves are driven by the parochial charges to the verge of pauperism. (Standard, 5th April, 1867) [49].

Frightful spectacles were seen many parts of England. It was 40,000 of them, they were unemployed, helpless, starving, and dying.

The local ratepayers themselves were driven by the parochial charges to the verge of pauperism. They were sufferers, terrible, and out of a job. They cried their misery in peoples' ears, they cried to Heaven, and they told citizens from their miserable dwellings. It was useless for them. At any time, they could be killed by disease, hunger, and poor dwelling.

They needed help and rescue. They begged but the results were fruitless. In many countries of the present world, a similar scenario can be seen. Garcin also begged to open the door for help but Valet didn't open. He returned to hell. Whatever development, or technology, we invented, stomach cry can be heard. A million people died of English disease.

Fear Power

Most countries' economic strength is measured by reserve money or gold. Over uses reserve currency and drain of gold is a bad signs of the economic position of the country. At the time of over-drain of gold and foreign currency, bank or the government interrupt the market. Sometimes issues Act to stop the drain. According to Adam Smith, the market must be free. Out of governments interruptions—that is a free market. He argues that the market has maintenance power. Demand and supply naturally control all kinds of crises. It is the belief ideology of a free market policy.

"Fear is a powerful emotion" Osinakchi Akuma Kalu writes [50]. *Fear is the power of all power.*

We have seen the power of cats. Can a cat fight with a man? It doesn't dare to fight but in fear, it fights. A thief cannot run and jump from a height. In fear, he can do what he cannot do in a fearless time.

Plenty of such examples we have. Normally we look at its weak part, we never see the Hercules and Bhima part. Fear—in it's important form is Hercules and Bhima.

The new nobility was the child of its time, for which money was the power of all powers [51]. Marx focused, on money as the power of all powers. I reject it. And it was first rejected by Aristotle. My argument is the power of all power is not money; fear is one step bigger and earlier than it.

At a time of famine and pandemic, money can do nothing. In a state of fear, no one had money. Everyone had fear. That fear developed society, politics, invention, creation, and money, and saved a human generation.

Power is not counted as an emotion. Fear is the first emotion. It has a dual character; *via* the mind and the brain. All emotions including fear come from the emotion store. Special Fear comes from the brain. So, it is not an exaggeration that *fear is a superpower*. In practice, it can be seen. The collective fears minimize the power of the enemy. Society is the collective power of fear, not the collective fear of power. When we started to live in a group, it became power. Eventually, that became a nation.

Devendra Shakten writes, "Fearism is like an epic in which it has got cognition of everything of everywhere. Its every chapter and subtitles are logical, comparative, true proverbs and intellectual analysis filled with slogan-like sentences. Fear arises in each animal with internal materials consciousness. Fear emerges with consciousness and knowledge, and it is a living flame of insight consciousness. It was yesterday, it is even today and will be tomorrow too" [52].

Alexandre Kelsick, opinions "In his treatise on 'Transphilosophism', the philosopher Desh Subba argues that human nature is essentially emotive and that the primary driving emotion in human affairs is, fear. Subba engages in a sweeping critique of the Western philosophical tradition and argues that all ideologies and conceptual structures are rooted in fear. In this synoptic analysis of Subba's work, I shall expose the reductionism in his thinking. For while I agree, as do most credible modern philosophers including Heidegger, that human nature is essentially emotive, I question Subba's claim that fear is the root-emotion guiding human behaviour [53]. Obviously, there are yeah and nay-sayers regarding my philosophy of fearism and this conception of fearmorphosis at the base of human evolution and humanity.

Pure capital is a morsel of the financial enterprise. To reach to mountain-top, Homer has given;

> There I saw Sisyphus in infinite moan.
> With both hands heaving up a massy stone.
> And on his tip-toes racking all his height.
> To wrest up to a mountain-top his freight;

All the time capitalists encounter turmoil. The risk is always on the way to the vertex. He has to heave up with both hands and multiple heads (ideas). The crisis of raw materials, labour problems, the banking system, and high competition are the slope on the way to the peak. Those are successful, who penances as Bhageeratha. His effort didn't succeed at one time. He penanced 1000 years and one year living only on air. That's why his effort became very popular in the Indian continent as Bhageeratha labour.

The banking discount rate, still 3 to 3.5% in January 1847, rose to 7% in April, when the first panic broke out. The situation eased somewhat in the summer (6.5%, 6%), but when the new crop failed as well panic broke out afresh and even more violently [54].

In 1847 the first economic panic broke out. Failed of the new crop was the reason for it. During that time, the economy was based on the crop. Even today, many countries' economy and GDP is based on agriculture. When it broke out, it affected the discount rate of the bank. While the backbone fractures, panic arise in the country. At present, we can observe, the Ukraine war raised panic in the economy and foodstuffs around the globe.

"When a panic exists a man does not ask himself what he can get for his bank-notes, or whether he shall lose one or two percent by selling his exchequer bills, or three percent. If he is under the influence of alarm he does not care for the profit or loss, but makes himself safe and allows the rest of the world to do as they please" [55].

It is a report by first-rate export, the esteemed crafty Quaker, Samuel Gurney, of Overend, Gurney, and Co. At the alarm, there is no competition for profit, they compete to survive; everything goes to the corner. This case doesn't apply only in London, it is fit everywhere. Somehow, a man wants to survive. He doesn't care for anything unless he's safe.

At the normal time, a capitalist says money...money and money. "Time is money" as said by R, Michael Fisher [56]. At the alarm, money, money, and money change into life, life, and life. They abandon all their money and save their life. Even a man doesn't care about family members. First, he wants to save, and after his survival comes family members.

I give a practical example. In 2015, a big earthquake was in Nepal. Two friends were talking in the room. Suddenly appeared an earthquake. Young boys ran out to save their life. When they were saved, then they remembered, mother was inside the room. They left her there. Some people who were in the hotel room naked came out. They forgot to wear clothes.

The following extracts are also taken from the Parliamentary Report on Commercial Distress, 1847-48.—Owing to the crop failure and famine of 1846-47 large-scale imports of foodstuffs became necessary. "These circumstances caused the imports of the country to be very largely in excess over...exports. A considerable drain upon the banks, and an increased application to the discount brokers.... for the discount of bill..... They began to scrutinise the bill...The facilities of houses then began to be very seriously curtailed, and the weak houses began to fail. Those houses which relied upon their credit,.. went down. This increased the alarm that had been previously felt; and the bankers and others finding that they would not rely with the same degree of confidence that they had previously done upon turning their bills and other money securities into bank-notes, for the purpose of meeting their engagement, still further curtailed their facilities, and in many cases refused them together, they locked-up their bank-notes, in many instances to meet their own engagement; they were afraid of parting with them…The alarm and confusion were increased daily; and unless Lord John Russell.. had issued the letter to the Bank…universal bankruptcy would have been the issue.. (pp.74-75) [57].

It is taken from the parliamentary Report on Commercial Distress, 1847-48.—Owing to the crop failure and famine of 1846-47 large-scale imports of foodstuffs became necessary. The famine killed many citizens. In this crisis, the priority went to rescue life. The country made an import policy rather than an export. They began to scrutinize the bill…The facilities of houses then began to be very seriously curtailed, and the weak houses began to fail. They cut off the excess bill and save for the import of foodstuff. Such a crisis alarmed them seriously. Everyone had to be serious; that serious was for the rescue life. Foodstuff became the primary concern rest went secondary. Food became more valuable than diamonds and the value of the money went into the rubbish paper. When the Samsa family had a food shortage, Gregor's sister and mother sold their jewels. In several places above we read about, a husband who sold his wife and children when he had a crisis. Whatever we have and do, in case of a food crisis, we do not pay attention to miscellaneous but concentrated on food. The existence precedes essence and the existence of fear precedes essence varies like the sky and the earth.

The rise in the rate of profit has been in consequences of the rise in commodity-prices by speculation, is a logical absurdity, etc., That anything can ultimately destroy its own cause is a logical absurdity only for the usurer enamoured of the high interest rate [58].

Of course, anything can ultimately destroy its own cause. That is called self-hell. The destruction of Hitler was his own cause. If we see global warming, pollution, and extinction of species, these are happening because of human causes. Ecological destruction means ultimately the destruction of the human species.

At last, we are being scapegoated for our doings. We are making our hell. This hell is made by us, not by other people.

Gregor Samsa's hell is made by family members. In life of Kafka, his life was hell by his father (and other people). Such come under 10%, 90% is made by self.

First, we scapegoated ecology, and later we victimized. It can be applied to every sphere of life. The rise in the rate of profit had been in consequence of the rise in commodity prices by speculation, which was logical. Only for the usurer enamoured of the high-interest rate was a logical absurdity. It can be applied to capital, politics, and individuals.

"And why does he want to obtain the command of a greater quantity of capital? Because he wants to employ that capital; and why does he want to employ that capital? Because it is profitable to him to do so; it would not be profitable to him to do so if the discount destroyed his profit [59].

A concept of a greater quantity of capital is similar to the sky water of Bhageeratha. A philosophical question started with why does he want to obtain the command of a greater quantity of capital? Marx's answer was that he wants to employ that capital and make it profitable.

We need to trace the origination of capital. Locke said, "Man by nature is a property-acquired animal." All the quotes of philosophers come from the why because their answer didn't reach the origin.

In the barbarian, starvation was the big crisis. To solve it, a hunter-gathering society was formed. Hunting was not a permanent solution. They produced crops, vegetables and started to sell. The capitalist wanted more capital and profit because he was afraid of Tartarus boulder. Why did they want to obtain the capital? Why did they obtain money? The reason was fear of the infernal world. Everyone wanted to enjoy Shangri-la life.

Since property here exists in the form of stock, its movement and transfer become purely a result of gambling on the stock exchange, where the little fish are swallowed by the sharks and the lambs by the stock-exchange wolves [60].

Farming without land was impossible. In farming-gambling, whoever won got crops, and whoever lost got nothing. The gambler might lose the stake (life).

Normally little fish are swallowed by the sharks and small animals are hunted by the big. The small animal, the small investor always panics from the big. The hierarchy of scapegoats can be applied here. It means those who had more capital, could hunt small. Normally it happens in the capitalist market.

Once my friend told me, he won the tender for a coffee shop, near Star Ferry, Hong Kong, later Pacific Cafe paid double the rent and grabbed it from his mouth. All the time small fish and lambs are afraid of being eaten by big and biger fear—that is, defeat in the competition. It is fear play. Stockbrokers are always alert like frightened deer.

C. Fearmorphosis

On Colonisation

The major task of colonialists was to scapegoat the feeble nations. To attack them they use all kinds of ideas. The colonists tried their best, in retrospect, with problems, to save the nation and its people.

Sisyphus wanted to save Ephyra from a drought. Gregor wanted to save his family even at the last moment.

The colonist had been economically drained and had a drought of money. They needed money to irrigate the dry part of the economy. The internal sources were not abundant. The production quantity was increased. The local market couldn't consume large production, and they required a new market. Colonization was a new market for them. They scapegoated the colonized and made fertile land.

The colonizer confuses the form of supply with the supply itself and believes that society hitherto lived from hand to mouth or trusted to the hap of the morrow [61].

Society had always hand-to-mouth problems. Fear Sisyphus rammed a boulder from an early time. It was his hap according to Camus. He has written many places on hap of marrow in his essay. Sisyphus was the output of it. I have given my standpoint that fear precedes hap of marrow. Hand-to-mouth crisis links to it.

Finally, it is a striking fact that Adam Smith forgets to mention labour-power when counting off the constituent parts of the circulating capital [62].

It was not a question of Adam Smith forgetting to mention labour-power when counting off the constituent parts of the circulating capital. The very important part was fear of labour and capitalist. Of course, when we looked at the 'Wealth of the Nation' from Das Capital's critical angle, labour-power was missing. Without it, capital could not operate.

"The form, however, is of no consequence. The various kinds of food clothing, and shelter, necessary for the existence and comfort of the human being, are also changed. They are consumed, from time to time, and their value reappearance" [63].

The basic need for existence and comfort of human beings, is changed according to time and space. It doesn't mean our need changes. Need remains constant; it changes the forms of food, shelter, and clothing. Yesterday, we preferred hunting, at present we farm. Our fear and need are the same. The signifiers are changing it as stated by Albert Einstein.

"While the peasant farmer starves, his cattle thrive. Repeated showers had fallen in the country, and the forage was abundant. The Hindoo peasant will perish by hunger beside a fat bullock. The prescriptions of superstition, which appear cruel to the individuals, are conservative for the community; and the preservation of the labouring cattle secures the power of cultivation, and the sources of future life and wealth. It may sound harsh and sad to say so, but in India, it is more easy to replace a man than an ox" [64].

According to Marx, the position of the peasant was lower than an ox in India. Religious, superstition and conservative beliefs were in its support. This sentence says that farmers were not dying by starvation, they were killed by superstition and conservative. It was in the past and in the present too. They were scapegoated. Even the Hindoo peasant perished of hunger beside a fat bullock, he didn't leave belief. It was fixed. They were afraid that 'when I leave God, society will punish me,' they thought. They were feared the conservative community.

The degree of traditional fear was more than hunger. SSS is nailed in the heart. It can be read in SSS. What did constitute the structure of the self-immolation of the Sati system? Double fear conducts them to self-immolation into the pyre of their deceased husband. It is also applicable to Hindoo peasants. When reading Gregor Samsa's pain and stress; it was smaller than family maintenance. So, he wanted to go to work, though he was vermin.

In them nature does nothing; man does all; and the reproduction must always be in proportion to the strength of the agents that occasion it [65].

It is my argument that nature never selects and helps us in decisions as said by Darwin. Neither it is as said by Sartre. Sartre said we make a decision through our choice and selection. Fear is the decision-making factor. We had many cards in the state of nature. Fear structured society and fostered it. Nature was silent. Fearmorphosis is the fundamental process.

Labour-power is indeed his property (every self-renewing, reproductive), not his capital. It is the only commodity which he can and must sell continually in order to live, and which acts as capital (variable) only in the hands of the buyer, the capitalist [66].

Marx didn't apparently write it, he hinted. Labourer had one commodity that was himself. In case of option available, he didn't sell. At once a man became a slave because of his commodity. Even today in many countries, we find semi-slaves. Employees can categorize as semi-slave because they sell their commodity for a certain hour. At that time, they are not free. Either classical slave or, present employee fright is central.

This brilliant analysis is quite worthy of that deep thinker who copies on the one hand from Adam Smith that "labour is the source of wealth" (p. 242) that the industrial capitalists "employ their capital to pay for labour that reproduces it with a profit" (p. 246); and who concluded on the other hand that these industrial capitalists "feed all the other people, are the only ones who increase the public wealth, and create all our means of employment" (p. 242) that it is not the capitalists who are fed by the labourers, but the labourers who are fed by the capitalists. Why? For the brilliant reason that the money with which the labourers are paid does not remain in their hands, but continually returns to the capitalists in payment of the commodities produced by the labourers [67].

An allegation by Marx and Engels; the money with which the labourers are paid does not remain in their hands, and continually returns to the capitalists. It is a circle M (money). Labourer comes first or the capitalist and meantime, money starts to circulate from the hand of labourer or capitalist. We need to find the genesis of money, labour, and capital. Everyone was labourer at first. It begins with Adam, Eve, and Manu. A man was a nomad. Before marked a piece of land, his property was himself. After having land, they transformed it into commodities. After a long time, Adam Smith said, "Labour is the source of wealth", and the industrial capitalists "employ their capital to pay for labour that reproduces it with a profit," and came the time of, "feed all the other people, are the only ones who increase the public wealth, and create all our means of employment".

Whatever, Marx, Engels, and the present capitalist say, that origination of capital came from fear. It can be read in Satan, Adam and Eve. Even today, we can experience, that when we lose a job or business, first we fear its consequences.

As far back as October 1855, Leonard Homer complained about the resistance of very many manufacturers to the legal requirements concerning safety devices on horizontal shafts, although the danger was continually emphasized by accidents, many of them fatal, and although these safety devices did not cost much and did not interfere with production [68].

Leonard Homer was afraid that labourers may die in any accidents. It was necessary to take precautions. Safety devices were not costly. It was the cause he complained about the resistance of manufacturers to the legal requirements concerning safety devices. In every sector of life, we emphasize safety rules, and safety equipment to protect our life. In 1855 Homer drew attention that manufacturers must follow the safety rules. We can see safety rules in house, car, working place, public transport, etc.

At present, confidence is not only restored after the panic of 1857, but the panic itself seems to be almost forgotten [69].

It depends on the effect of an earthquake. A low-scale earthquake vibrates for a short time but a high scale vibrates for a long time. There was a high vibrate economic panic in 1857. It trembled for quite a long but it was restored after some time. The panic is also the same. A high level of panic vibrates for a long time, a short vibrate short, and forgets later. We can experiment with it in the wound. At bleeding, we panic, after a while it stops, and we forget. The wound of 1857 was almost forgotten after some years.

Gyges Ring and Panopticon

The concept of Gyges Ring is given in *The Republic* of Plato. During a philosophical discussion with Socrates, Glaucon mentioned it. He asked, "If somebody has an invisible ring can he behave just because he can commit crimes and vanish?" People want to hide, after doing illegal activities. They feared the various Panopticon surveillance them. Sisyphus hid for a long time in Ephyra. Later Mercury came and took him to hell. He then falls into the clutches of the usurer, and once in the usurer's power he can never extricate himself [70].

The usurer's clutches were very strong in medieval Europe. Once they clutched it, it was hard to extricate. Was there any chance to extricate from the mouth of the Mammon? Was it possible for

Sisyphus? It can be applied in the case of a poor country, people even today. Once a poor country is clutched by the colonialist, it is hard to extricate. In the Roman Empire, a man sold his wife, children, and himself. Sisyphus has enslaved in the Odyssey. In Camus's words, he was a proletarian in front of the usurer. In Kafka's words, he is Gregor Samsa.

Fifteen years ago I took pen in hand against usury when it had spread so alarmingly that I could scarcely hope for any improvement [71].

The author had taken pen in hand against usury when it had spread so alarmingly. The peasants had a hard to pay the interest of the usurer. The usury business was very worse for peasants. It scapegoated many people. Many people were left with anxiety, mental pressure, hypertension, and depression. The high rate of interest imposed on them. They mentally tortured customers.

Mere "anxiety" as Heidegger says, is at the source of everything [72]. Fearism believes that anxiety is a part of fear. As said by Heidegger, anxiety is not the source of everything. It starts with fear and ends with fearlessness. We can remove fear and experiment with it. We can see the consequences.

At present, the form of usurer has transformed into a financial institute, money laundering, investment, loan, bank, etc., they offer a loan, credit, and instalment but at the time of repayment, if unable to pay, they mentally and physically torture. It is the reason, many people do suicide, are depressed, go anxious, and mentally stressed. It answered the philosophical question of Camus. They seek to find Gyges ring. They think they are always under surveillance by the lender's Panopticon.

Capital starts from raw material, labour, production, and at the end sale of the product were steps of capitalism. It needs many steps. Collectively, we can call it, the mechanization of capital. The factory has one mechanization, raw material to finished product. Finish product to capital has another mechanization. The first and second mechanization reach the capital stage. The next process is capital to capital. First Capital is raw capital for finished capital. In this capital-to-capital process, some scapegoat, and some Panopticon plays a role but Sisyphus heaves up his freight as said by Homer.

So far as it is based on a high rate of surplus value, a high rate of profit is possible when the working day is very long, although labour is not highly productive [73].

We can take a good example from present companies. In developing and developed countries, generally people work 10 hours per day. In underdeveloped countries (particularly for government employees), yet, 10 hours is just the notion of their working hours. Most actually work hard for 5 hours. They rest 5 hours drinking tea, talking, moving around, gossiping, and having lunch breaks. Why do they demonstrate careless, mainly because they have no fear of a code of conduct, rule, and punishment. Also, once they recruit for the job, they are concrete there. It is hard to remove them. In developed countries, at least they work 8 hours, and 2 hours they take breaks. They worry about termination and punishment. So, how many hours a day they work, is not an issue, but how to be liable for their personal, superior, and the law, is an issue.

How much the individual capitalist must bear of the loss, i.e., to what extent he must share in it at all, is decided by strength and cunning, and competition then becomes a fight among hostile brothers [74].

Individual capitalists always do the competition and fight among hostile brothers. They use strength and cunning to win the game. Animals also play the game over the food, but they use natural cunning, fear, and power. Human uses persuasion, purchase, punishment, and exploitation to overcome the battle.

Human history unfolds, and that's why the thesis, antithesis, and synthesis of fear. Thesis, antithesis, and synthesis were first explained in Samkhya philosophy (The date of Samkhya is unclear) in the name of Sattva, Rajas, and Tamas; second Socrates, third Hegel, fourth Marx, and fifth Subba. The rotation of the process is thesis, antithesis, and synthesis.

It is self-evident from what has gone before that nothing could be more absurd than to regard merchant's capital, whether in the shape of commercial or money-dealing capital, as a particular variety of industrial capital, such as, say, mining, agriculture, cattle-raising, manufacturing, transport, etc., which are side-lines of industrial capital occasioned by the division of social labour, and hence different spheres of investment [75].

Industrial capital was invested in agriculture, cattle-raising, manufacturing, mining, and transport on the side-lines. These were steps of our needs and civilization. Neither our steps nor civilization proceeded to ignore subsistent issues. The capital and investments followed it. In starvation, buyers didn't buy transport. In this trend came agriculture followed by cattle-raising. Cattle raising was earlier than agriculture. Different spheres of investments followed that. These were metamorphoses of capital. In fact, these were not side-line businesses. It was a core line. On this basis, capital developed as side-lines.

The trade of the first independent flourishing merchant towns and trading nations rested as a pure carrying trade upon the barbarism of the producing nations, between whom they acted the middleman [76].

In historically spheres of investments extended, one can see various stages of colonization. The East India Company is an example of that merchant acting as the middleman. First, it came to India and later, the British Government. British Government and British business flourished all over the Indian continent.

It is in the nature of things that as soon as town industry has many, it separates from agricultural industry, its products are from the outset commodities and thus require the mediation of commerce for their sale—leaning the commerce towards the development of towns, and, on the other hand, the dependence of towns upon commerce, are so far natural [77].

The Merchant flourished step by step. First, their production and market were in small villages and jumped to towns. As soon as the town industry separated from the agricultural, its products were from the outset commodities and thus required the mediation of commerce for their sale. At present, we have many agents, mediators, and middlemen. They facilitated all kinds of markets, merchants, and capitals.

There is no doubt, and it is precisely this fact which has led to wholly erroneous conceptions that in the 16th and 17th centuries the great revolutions, which took place in commerce with the geographical discoveries and speeded the development of merchant's capital, constitute one of the principal elements in furthering the transition from feudal to capitalist mode of production [78].

The 16th and 17th centuries were the great revolutions, which took place not only in commerce but also in all spheres of life. It was the transition from a feudal to a capitalist. People were looking for alternatives to feudalism. What was the cause of the 16th and 17th centuries' great revolutions? Liberty was the cause. Cats wanted to be free. It was combined with two mentalities. A large number of people were hell by the minority. They were in poverty and had difficulties. So, their interest was free from the cage, as said by Gerald C. Maccallum Jr..

Metamorphosis manv camouflages according to time and space. Otherwise, it goes extinct from existence. Hunting, agriculture, and capitalism are camouflage forms of civilization.

Shylock

Usurpation is a business operations, the same as other businesses. In the Marxist's eye, every business looked the Shylock and Mammon who heaved-up freight. I don't see them in every business. It is an idea and tip-toes racking all the height.

Anyone wrests up to a mountain-top his freight. Labour-power is not exceptional. Yes, design, quantity, and quality are dissimilar. Labour does overtime for extra income. Salesboy Samsa did the same for 15 years. Shylock invests for more interest. He is a cruel money lender according to William Shakespeare. The capitalists invest for more profit. However, they are racking toil their freight. Gregor's employer did the same.

We assume, then, that agriculture is dominated by the capitalist mode of production just as manufacture is; in other words, that agriculture is carried on by capitalists who differ from other capitalists primarily in the manner in which their capital, and the wage-labour set in motion by this capital, are invested [79].

Ancestors were first in hunting, then agriculture, and agriculture was metamorphosed to the mode of capitalists.

Within capitalism, several systems developed. The proletariat Sisyphus rams up his boulder to the agricultural slope to the capitalist mountain-top. In this movement, Gregor Samsa(es) metamorphosis into various vermin. Subsistence was the cause of the metamorphosis. It is a part of advancement.

Nearly the whole of the dock accommodation in our seaport towns is by the same process of usurpation in the hands of the great leviathan of the land [80]. The great leviathan is a symbol of a sea monster. Usurpation was the Shylock and Mammon in a money lending. In the industrial revolution, Shylock was Elise. The fact is if the usurpation system was permitted to be in full operation for a considerable period, the house, and property would be in their capture. Nearly the dock accommodation in seaport towns was held by them in the same process of usurpation.

Ground-rent so capitalised constitutes the purchase price or value of the land, a category which like the price of labour is *prima facie* irrational, since the earth is not the product of labour and therefore has no value [81].

The earth has no value in terms of money. It is natural. A man added to the value of the land. So, a man deserved added value. In agriculture, its value raised, but still, it is rising because people are farming property market in the land at present.

This is precisely what a usurer would do under similar circumstances, with just the difference that the usurer would at least risk his own capital in the operation [82]. The usurer was always alert, at any time sinks his investment ship. Once almost it happened to Antonio. His ships could not return on time. He had to pay flesh from body parts to Shylock. Everyone wanted to save their investment.

Interest was their boulder. Today, we have many Shylocks in the name of financial institutions.

The increase in rental is evidence of a public disaster [83].

The capital runs in a chain. Any chain is lost, rushed, and damaged, it collapses the pyramid building. The rent is a part of it. An increase in rent, it calls a public disaster. At this moment, terror smoked their air. The rent and bank interest had interlinked. When interest increases in the USA, it badly affects the world economy. It was the same in the 19th century in England.

One of the biggest Shylocks is the high tax system of the country. Most of the developed countries impose a high tax rate. Tax is their breath and food. It suffocates people's life. In another term, it makes many scapegoats.

Every year in the budget speech, tax is an important part of the fiscal year. Undeveloped countries are freer. They enjoy more freedom of tax.

Many businessmen, and celebrities, want to hide under Gyges Ring. If they get this ring they are definitely invisible. The smart strategic government uses the secret Panopticons to find them. In this case, George Harrison wrote a song "Taxman" and became invisible for some time in England. It is happening all over the world. It is a part of capitalism the usuer game.

Businessmen, celebrities, and rich men leave the country and migrate to low-tax countries. Revenue is the main income source of the country. Developed and capitalist countries' political agendas always consist of the tax. When we observe the presidential candidate of the US and the prime minister candidate of the UK their manifesto typically highlights the tax.

B. Maria Kumar and R. Fisher write, "Capitalism also brought its own fears in the guise of celebrated competition and 'exchange' economics over the traditional 'gifting' economies of earlier societies; any economic scenario based on a competitive climate is usually tinged with anxiety and fear....It was George Harrison of 'The Beatles' who wrote a bitter song named 'Taxman' way back in 1966 about how much tax money their group was paying to the British government then. Fear of taxes ultimately drove the rock band to leave their country…in protest, although not permanently [84].

These writers thus take as their point of departure a situation where, in the first place, the agricultural population still constitute the overwhelming majority of the nation, and, secondly, the landlord still appears as the person appropriating at the first hand the surplus-labour of the direct producers by virtue of his monopoly of landed property, where landed property, therefore; still appears as the main condition of production [85].

How we develop technology, the farmers cannot ignore. Our basic needs cannot be fulfilled by technology. The technologies are subordinates. It assists in production. So, the agricultural population still constitutes most of the nation. All activities are around the appetite. Thus writers took it as their prime departure. The scenario of production, industry, and capitalism was changing. At present, most of the nations are running under Sotalism.

The physiocrats are troubled by difficulties of another nature [86]. In the 18th century, the situation was rapidly changing. The agriculture trade was shifting. An advanced form of agriculture was developing. Trade and business metamorphosed into a free market and globalization. Because of these reasons, the physiocrats faced another Pandora. They were in chains. One drop of black ink affects all water in the jar. The chain is similar to a drop of black ink. Their major Pandora was an existential crisis. They were afraid of the extinction of identity.

As a transitory form of the original form of rent to capitalist rent, we may consider the metayer system, or share-cropping, under which the manager (farmer) furnishes labour (his own or another's), and also a portion of working capital, and the landlord furnishes, aside from land, another portion of working capital (e.g., cattle), and the product is divided between tenant and landlord in definite proportions which vary far from country to country [87].

Metayer system is still running in many countries. It was one of the best in the feudal system. In this system, the manager (farmer) furnished labour (his own or another's), and also a portion of working capital, and the landlord furnished, aside from land, another portion of working capital (e.g., cattle), and the product was divided between tenant and landlord in definite proportions which vary far from country to country. It helped those who had no land for farming. The landlord invested his capital in the land. Capitalization was the advanced form of metayer.

It is an enchanted, perverted, topsy-turvy world, in which Monsieur le Capital and Madame la Terre do their ghost-walking as social characters and at the same time directly as mere things [88].

Beautiful dancing words are here; it is an enchanted, perverted, topsy-turvy world. Capital as Mr. and Earth as Madam, do catwalk ghost-walking in the civilization stage. In other words, they are Prakriti and Purush. Earth and capital both have an important part in consciousness and freedom.

The Geist wants freedom and full consciousness. The first Prakriti (soul) of Kapilmuni desired to expose. To expose it, one joins Purush. The capitalist wants to be free from fear. Its combined word is Metaidealism, which is first written in *Trans Philosophism* [89].

SYNOPSIS OF STORIES

We have no bigger God, Demon, and capital than *appetite*. The Olympic of life runs from here. It is our Olympia. Appetite motivates. It explores the destination. Destinations are set by it.

If we count words one by one in Das Capital, the number of means of subsistence is always higher. The synonym of the story is the means of subsistence. With appetite, all parts of the organ contribute to subsistence. In the capital market, raw materials to profit, and various mechanisms are working through it. Either capital market or function of the body's parts—appetite is equal to survival.

The highest activity of survival is the means of subsistence. So, the capital story declares and accepts, our story is the story of survival.

I re-vision it because the means of subsistence is marginal in Das Capital. Krishna is all the way in Mahabharat. Similarly, in the *Iliad* and *Odyssey*, Homer is all the way.

It means that the story, sub-story, and chapters we read in *Iliad* and *Odyssey*, are an image of Homer. His presence is from beginning to end—all there. But the form is invisible. In *Das Capital*, whatever we read, moves around means of subsistence. It is like Mahabharat because Krishna is there from beginning to end.

Means of subsistence is a major articulating thematic character in the capital story and our life. The Olympic flame runs on its base. The game plays in its stadium. To give justice to it, I've brought fearmorphosis.

We can see the 21st century movie on the latest version monitor. It is not a new release, it is a historical movie. The stages of strides were step by step. Our age is like the mountain-top. Means of subsistence rock is pushed from generation to generation. We are a continuation of our ancestors and legacy. Our mountain-top relies on Sisyphus, the means of subsistence is our stone. We are rolling it from very early.

Das Capital is a boulder of Karl Marx. His mountaineer team has step by step heaved up a boulder. All the way fear of falling is in their mind. At present, it is falling in many countries. Some countries' economy has been crushed by rock, and people face the threat. It is the stone of the 21st century, we are developed Sisyphus.

Whether barbarian or advanced Sisyphus, our freight is the same. Exactly we are ramming the same load since the beginning. Whether capitalists or workers, they ram up subsistence. The capitalist is also a coolie, only the form and load are different. Is the richest man not pushing a stone and doesn't have the risk of being crushed? He rolls himself more than his freight. He is the Mammon Sisyphus manv.

Karl Marx focused on the labourer. I use equalitarian, either the boulder of the Shylock or the rock of the proletariat Sisyphus. One thing is very common, they cannot buy eternal breath. One day, they have to pause their stone. The stone waits for another Sisyphus, similar to when Sisyphus went to the underworld a second time, the rock was waiting for him.

We are pushing ourselves, generation, culture, language, religion, myth, belief, agriculture, and capital. People call it development. I call it metamorphosis caused by fearmorphosis.

Sisyphus's stone cannot segment, but the capitalist rock can segment. Flakes of rock formed the story. Das Capital interprets the silent sound of perpetuating life. Fearmorphosis speaks a bit loudly.

We are acting in survival. The chapters close at the time when we stop breathing. Our every move is for the protection, preservation, security, and conservation of life. Every move of Chess is to protect the king. When the king dies the game is over. Das Capital's name is given by Karl Marx. I saw the embryo of fearmorphosis in its womb.

Its production consequently pre-supposes his existence. Given the individual, the production of labour-power consists in his reproduction of himself or his maintenance. For his maintenance, he requires a given quantity of the means of subsistence. Therefore the labour-time requisite for the production of labour-power reduces itself to that necessary for the production of those means of subsistence. In other words, the value of labour-power is the value of the means of subsistence necessary for the maintenance of labourer.

Labour-power, however, becomes a reality only by its exercise; it sets itself in action only by working. But thereby a definite quantity of human muscle, nerve, brain, etc., is wasted, and these require restoration of some degree.

This increased expenditure demands a large income. "If the owner of the labour-power works today, tomorrow he must again be able to repeat the same process in the same conditions as regards health and strength. His means of subsistence must therefore be sufficient to maintain him in his normal state as a labouring individual. His natural wants, such as food, clothing, fuel, and housing, vary according to the climatic and other physical conditions of his country" [90].

It is a synopsis of the story and Marxism. Existence is the primary concern of human beings and animals. The human being uses their rational skills and labour to maintain it. When they lack natural resources, they use their Bhageeratha. This labour-power is in the form of commodities and products. They can sell it and maintain their life.

In society, they are not a single person. They have family and society. Until they have options, they don't necessarily sell it. Their last option is selling off their private property. Even though they are not willing to sell, Pandora forces them.

Once they sell it, for the time being, they converted into a bull, ox, buffalo, horse, and donkey to push, pull, and carry a load. Sometimes transformed into a dog. The dog has to watch and secure the master. Long hair, unclear voice, flat ear, patched nose, and walking with four legs; are their Gregor Samsa form.

They lose their freedom. They have no choice. As a living commodity, they must full-fill the capitalist desire that belongs to them. They are doing all this for food, clothing, and housing. If basic needs are not abundant, there's a high chance of immature death. They are fear Sisyphus, who repeats the same process every day, the owner of the labour-power works today, and tomorrow they must again be able to repeat the same process.

The hunting, the feudal, the industrial age, and finally capital age are forms of Gregor Samsa. As the Prakirti, fear is continuously traveling with us. In another language, we are a boulder of fear.

Sometimes going up to the peak and sometimes rolling down. This repetition is called Historical Fearism. We never stop rolling it and/or fear never stops rolling us.

Sotalism is a mountain-top, it again rolls down. From time to time it is happening to the capital market. Between boulder and Sisyphus, exists means of subsistence. When stopping the supply of it, a stone and Sisyphus pauses as the statue of the universe.

A labourer sells his property for subsistence. Subsistence is the prime concern. His existence always comes along with labour business. Nevertheless, he doesn't sell him. Marx's labour-power term is vague. Labour-power, skill, expertise, talent, and genuineness are different. Labour-power is simply the Sisyphus and Bhageeratha brand. 19th century, employees didn't push as Sisyphus and penance as Bhageeratha. At present, the number of such employees is fewer and skilled Sisyphus are more because the ratio of competition is higher.

Shirts, for instance, are a necessary means of subsistence, but are only one out of many [91]. A cloth was a basic need for life. Primitive forms of garments were bark and leaves, etc. It is also written in the Bible when Adam and Eve sinned, animals were killed by God to provide clothing for them (Genesis 3:21). According to the weather, our ancestors developed varieties of dresses. Whatever design and form, we had its basic objective was to protect life from bad weather. Many lives had been taken away by environmental conditions when protection was insufficient against it.

If a question be asked them, they never raised their eyes from their work from fear of losing a single moment [92].

Had Sisyphus raised his eyes when he was pushing a boulder? His situation was fearful because at any moment the boulder could have crushed him. So, he steadily pushed it. Labourers were similar to the King of Ephyra. Losing a single moment is very important in the Myth of Sisyphus and the story of Das Capital. Normally readers pay less attention to it whereas the whole universe is revolving around its base.

Let's see if asked questions employees, they never raise their eyes from their work. It is symbolic. It happens everywhere. The situation of a poor labourer is indicated here. An example was Mary Anne Walkley's case. Their liberty is based on behaviour, morality, and character of the employer. This situation may not see in the compassionate master. Raise their eyes or not it attaches to famine. Suppose an employer is graceful, they don't hesitate to raise their eyes but in the case of Kim Jong -Un, they fear to lift their eyes.

Finally, the majority of the members of society are transformed into wage-labourers, into people who live from hand to mouth, who receive their wages weekly and spend them daily, who therefore must have their means of subsistence made available to them in the shape of supply [93].

Whether labour or master they were transformed into different forms as the metamorphosis of butterflies. The growth of plants and man is metamorphous. If they don't metamorphose on time, they will die.

We cannot find perfect reason in the metamorphosis of Kafka and science. Science gives the definition, Kafka interprets Kafkaesque of it but does not give a reason. We are reading *Sisyphus* and *Metamorphosis* as prisoners of 'Allegory of the Cave.' Are we pigeonholed? Are we prisoners of confined meaning? No, we have freedom of meaning.

In the passage last quoted from Adam Smith, notice must also be taken of the following phrase: "A circulating capital which furnishes the maintenance of the workmen who make them" (machine, etc.) [94].

There is no doubt that Adam Smith highlighted the confined life of the workmen. Until the maintenance of the workmen, running capital was impossible. No one could work on a famished stomach. Did Camus and Sartre write and think with an empty stomach? The machine didn't run automatically.

When a savage makes bows, arrows, stone hammers, axes, baskets, etc., they know very well that they did not spend the time so employed in the production of articles of consumption, but that they had thus stocked up the means of production they need, and nothing else [95].

Normally, bows, arrows, stone hammers, axes, and baskets were used to keep going in life. It was a very useful tool in the *Homo sapiens* age. Still, it is in many indigenous communities. They were always exploring food. As a Fearism thinker, I look at it from different angles. First, these tools were made to reduce the fear of survivalist primal life. Second, it helped to stock up on the necessary foodstuff. When they had a store of food, they didn't have to worry about starvation, and immaturely dying. These tools worked as armor. Atomic and missile are its Trans Philosophism forms.

Nature there directly provides the means of subsistence, which need not first they produce. Nature thereby also gives to the primal person, who has but few wants to satisfy the time, not to use them as yet non-existent means of production in new production, but to transform, alongside the labour required to appropriate naturally existing means of production—that is, as other products of Nature into means of production: bows, stone knives, boats, etc. [96].

Nature gives life and it provides the means of subsistence, which need not first be produced. Everything runs smoothly. When consciousness-knowledge-fear activate at some point as central in a person's life, it seeks to rescue and explore for food.

In the beginning, Adam and Eve had no fear. After appeared Satan, it began. Many struggles encounter for subsistence. This fear activates, motivates, and insists to invent, create, and develop bows, stone knives, and boats. In history, biology, and linguistics, we could not find any other feeling than fear in the brain. It simultaneously links with other feelings. Among all activities, secure life is the priority. It is a real human story.

It is a large-scale industry, too, that thus finally conquers the domestic market for capital, puts an end to the small-scale production and natural economy of the self-sufficient peasant family, and places the entire nation in the service of capital [97].

Eventually, Marxism and their denunciation of capitalism, while showing the beauty of communism, is the new narrative. It blames the large-scale industry conquering the domestic market for capital, putting an end to small-scale production, and placing the entire nation in the service of capital. It is Marx's eye, and his eye is the enemy of capitalism. He ended up in large-scale industry. In the beginning, no one can be large-scale.

A person's fear spreads in different faculties of life. It seeks options. After experimenting, with several options, it reaches the best option.

We read, various parts of *The Myth of Sisyphus*, Hell is other people, The Allegory of Panopticon, The Myth of Scapegoat, Legend of Bhageeratha, Story of Das Capital, and *The Metamorphosis*. Not only these, but we also have narration, myth, religion, doctrine, and belief, and in the end, we reach life. Life always exists as central.

In the solar system, the sun throne in the middle, and planets and sub-planets revolve around its orbit. In life, life sits on the throne, all revolves in a circle.

According to Einstein, the speed of light changes time and space. In fearmorphosis, life uses time and space. A man is a narrator of the universe, earth, and an ecological destroyer. He is not a creator of nature but he is being created by it. Later metamorphoses into hell. We are living in the netherworld of Homer, Camus, and Sartre.

We all know that at the beginning of society, products are consumed by the producers themselves, and that these producers are spontaneously organized in more or less communistic communities; that the exchange of surplus of these products with strangers, which ushers in the conversation of products into communities, which is of a later date. We know that it takes places at the first only between individual communities of different tribes, but later also prevails within the community, and contributes considerably to the latter's dissolution into bigger or smaller family groups. But even after this dissolution, the exchange family heads remain working peasants, who produce almost all they require with the aid of their families on their own farmsteads and get only a slight portion of the required necessities from the outside in exchange of surplus products of their own.

The family is engaged not only in agriculture and livestock-raising; it also works their products up into finished articles of consumption. Now and then it even does its own milling with the hand-mill; it bakes bread, spins, dyes, weaves flax and wool, tans leather, builds and repairs wooden buildings, makes tools and utensils, and not infrequently does joinery and blacksmithing; so that the family, or family group, is in the main self-sufficient [98].

In history, we read there was a human. Later produced more people. They had no food stock, no house, and no weapons to kill animals. The walking person had a more dangerous and high risk to his life. They were a fear Sisyphus. Fear is a Sisyphus.

To reduce risk and fear, they started to walk in groups. First, one and plus one, and again added more. Adding process converted to society. Thus, we can understand, society was structured by Sisyphus(es). Gathering people became power. Society arranged means of basic needs in better ways.

In the beginning, transactions took place from person to person and later expanded to groups and communities. It is the form of development of society, and nation. In the course of time, basic needs changed accordingly. These forms were changing by needs; the family was engaged not only in agriculture and livestock-raising business; they also worked production up into finished; now and then it even does its own milling with the hand-mill; it bakes bread, spins, dyes, weaves flax and wool, tans leather, builds and repairs wooden buildings, makes tools and utensils, and not infrequently does joinery and blacksmithing; so that the family, or group, was in self-sufficient.

When the time was passing generation to generation and reached the Trans Philosophism age. A Sisyphus left a stone in a stair, and another Sisyphus continued, How far we walk, we are rooted in a single human. We are eight billion generations of single parents. We are a generation of ancestors [(Prakirti-Samkhya) (Spirit, idea, mind, reason, Geist-Hegel) (consciousness, fear-Subba)].

Life, market, and capital have a competitor. In this competition, a capitalist wants to earn more than a competitor. They apply many strategies to reach the mountain top. It relies on the circumstance.

All countries have been heaved up themselves and their capital. They are Sisyphus countries. They heave up their economy to the mountain-top, but that mountain-top never comes. In the name of capital; they heave up and down fear.

We are stone and we are Sisyphus. It is our hallucination but also reality that we are being watched by Panopticons. We are not mythical Sisyphus. A man is fear Sisyphus; being watched by Panopticons. The capital is a freight. We are rolling a boulder all the time. Sometimes rubs, and sometimes strikes. The rock is elastic; in hot increase and cold scrunch. Natural rock diminishes all the time, and one day reaches the dust. It reminds us of *The Old Man and The Sea*.

End Notes

1. https://kcsunbeam.wordpress.com/2022/07/14/trans-philosophism-book-review/
2. Marx and Engels (2015), p. 3.
3. Ibid.
4. Ibid., p. 8.
5. Ibid., p. 9.
6. Ibid., p. 10.
7. Ibid., p. 13.
8. Ibid., p. 15-6.
9. Camus (1955), p. 148.
10. Marx (1998/2021), p. 266.
11. Camus, p. 90.

12. https://www.academia.edu/82040476/Fearism
13. Discussed in detail in Subba (2021b), e.g., pp. 251, 254, 255, 260, 265.
14. Ibid., p. 433.
15. https://dazeinfo.com/2010/04/26/bhagiratha-who-brought-river-ganga-to-earth/
16. Marx (1998/2021), p. 17.
17. Ibid.
18. Ibid., pp. 36-7.
19. Ibid., p. 42.
20. Ibid.
21. https://en.wikipedia.org/wiki/History_of_money#cite_note-Graeber-68
22. Marx (1998/2021), p. 51.
23. Ibid., p. 94.
24. Ibid., p. 95.
25. Camus (1955), p. 89.
26. Marx, p. 115.
27. Ibid., 118.
28. Ibid., 131.
29. Ibid., 132.
30. Ibid., 139.
31. Marx (1998/2021), p. 151.
32. Ibid., pp. 155-6.
33. Ibid., pp. 160-1.
34. Camus (1955), p. 10.
35. Marx (1998/2021), p., 161.
36. https://www.actascientific.com/ASMS/pdf/ASMS-04-0593.pdf
37. Marx, p. 162.
38. Ibid., p. 291.
39. Ibid., pp. 297-8.
40. Ibid., p. 334.
41. Ibid., p. 350
42. Ibid., p. 359.
43. Ibid., p. 364.
44. Ibid., p. 365.
45. Ibid., p. 379.
46. Ibid., p. 394.
47. Ibid., p. 426.
48. Ibid., p. 427.
49. Ibid., pp. 435-6.
50. Kalu (2017), p. 96.
51. Marx (1998/2021), p. 477.
52. Rai (B.S. 2069).

53. https://www.academia.edu/98476957/Transphilosophism
54. Marx, p . 1071.
55. Ibid., p. 1075.
56. Fisher (2022).
57. Marx, p. 1077.
58. Ibid., p. 1081.
59. Ibid., p. 1083.
60. Ibid., p. 1084.
61. Ibid., p. 584.
62. Ibid., p. 627.
63. Ibid., p. 638.
64. Ibid., p. 646.
65. Ibid., p. 725.
66. Ibid., p. 773.
67. Ibid., p. 802.
68. Ibid., pp. 867-8.
69. Ibid., p. 888.
70. Marx, p. 1191.
71. Ibid., p. 1198.
72. Camus (1955), p. 10.
73. Ibid., p. 968.
74. Ibid., p. 972.
75. Ibid., p. 1017.
76. Ibid., p. 1020-21.
77. Ibid., p. 1021.
78. Ibid., p. 1022.
79. Marx (1998/2021), p. 1202.
80. (i.e., pp. 92-93); cited in Marx (1998/2021), p. 1205.
81. Ibid., p. 1206.
82. Ibid., p. 1208.
83. (*Du Mecanisime de Societe en France et en Angleterre,* by M. Rubichon, 2nd ed..Paris, 1837, p. 101) cited in Marx (1998/2021), p. 1210.
84. Fisher (2022), p. 73.
85. Marx, p. 1318.
86. Ibid.
87. Ibid., p. 1329.
88. Ibid., p. 1346.
89. Subba (2021b).
90. Marx (1998/2021), p. 108.
91. Ibid., p. 206.
92. Ibid., p. 288.
93. Ibid., p. 586.

94. Ibid., p. 630.
95. Ibid., p. 733.
96. Ibid., p. 1356.
97. Ibid., p. 1390
98. Ibid., p. 1385.

PART FIVE

NOVELEE GREGOR SAMSA

NOVELLA

The Metamorphosis is the masterpiece of Franz Kafka. I am looking at it from fearmorphosis basis.

How sincerely the young sales boy Gregor Samsa works for his family. Even though he was sick and became an insect still, worry and fear was haunting in his mind. We see how the family uses and throws him out.

Kafka has given a rigid fictional approach. We cannot see any reason for Gregor's transformation. Suddenly appeared like a curtain disclosed in *No Exit*. Otherwise, it needs a reason for the transformation. For instance, hunting life transformed into agriculture because of the food crisis. If there was no dearth of food, no need for metamorphosis. In time if they cannot metamorphosis, their life had high risk. It is the reason, from time to time, living creatures need metamorphosis.

Crawling, creeping, is a symbol of struggle. Gregor tried his best to be normal, and help his family. Transformation of fear can be observed here. To repeat the same process is a Sisyphus. When it mixes with fear, it transforms to fear Sisyphus. Its process is fearmorphosis. Fear morphosis is fearmorphosis. It is the process of metamorphosis of a living thing to save a life.

Before he had less fear. Members of the family were more or less fearless about finances. After his transformation, the level of fear increased; the fear of family increased because the income source was stopped.

After stopping income, morality, relations, honor, belief, behaviour, greeting, and respect transformed. As long as he had a good salary, everyone respected, greeted, believed, and honored him.

Gregor Samsa was Bhgeeratha. He thought about his job. It was necessary though he didn't like it. His father's debt was the main reason.

At any time Shylock might snatch his father as Sisyphus was seized by Mercury. If he is not to work, how is he to maintain house expenses? It was his tension. He wanted to wake up and go to work.

When he was vermin, he became the burden of the house. They wanted his death. Practically it happens in life. If a member is sick for a long time; it makes members tire of them. For example, coma, paralysis, handicapped, disabled, and mad.

His work was more important than his physical presence. When he had no job, no one liked him, everyone felt burdened.

Even if he is an insect, handicapped and old age; presume he holds property, pension, assets, or deposit, they love and care for him. Very rare chances of hating and ignoring. Another term we can say, they are not loving, or caring of a person; they care about money. It is applicable to the state too. Suppose useless animals suddenly became precious and started to make income, the nation claims its rights.

I divided the role of Gregor into employed and unemployed parts. In the first part, Gregor was lovely, friendly, and nice to everyone. He worked for 5 years without holidays. One night he transformed into an insect, and every member of the house went through some kind of metamorphous too.

A person is naturally transformed; the rest of the transformation is remuneration. It is appearance caused. Kafkaesque's cause is fear.

At the time, of good earnings, most of the fear disappears, and with no income, several fears appear. That's why good and bad relations depend on the degree of fear.

In the metamorphous process fear appears many forms. It does not merely happens in living things, but also happens in financial institutes, science, philosophy, language, and society as well.

Part One

Gregor Samsa is a member of the Samsa family. In the family, there are four members. Mr. Samsa is a retired employee. Mrs. Samsa is a housewife. His sister Grete Samsa is a 17-year young girl. She is learning violin. Mr. Samsa had a business five years before. The business was devasted and he has debt. No one had wages except Gregor. He was doing hard work to maintain family expenditures. The family was fully dependent on him. He loved them. He wanted to pay his father's debt. Thus, he worked hard. Grete and Madam Samsa took care of him. They were happy because he was earning.

Kafka writes, one morning, as Gregor Samsa was waking up from anxious dream, he discovered that in bed he had been changed into a monstrous vermin. He lay on his armour-hard back and saw, as he lifted his head up a little, his brown, arched abdomen divided up into rigid bow-like sections. From this height, the blanket, just about ready to slide off completely, could hardly stay in place. His numerous legs, pitifully thin in comparison to the rest of his circumference, flickered helplessly before his eyes [1].

When we simply look at his transformation, everything looks normal. When we dive a little deeper, we can see the mysterious and realistic lake; where we can see various creatures and their transformative forms. A monstrous vermin is a negative transformation. Nomadic life, the hunting age, the agriculture era, the industrial revolution, capitalism, and sotalism are positive transformations.

Kafka's life was similar to Gregor Samsa's life. He was always sick, and feeble. His father Hermann Kafka was very cruel and strict. He struggled hard to reach his mountain top. He wanted his son to be strong, brave, and successful. Whereas Kafka's life was the opposite. Because of fear of his father he didn't express problems. Once he got a punishment without any crime, then he transformed into a 'yes son'.

Before the last breath, he had a tear of love in his heart. Kafka delivers a message until a good income the family gives respect, love, greeting, and discipline. After losing a job, their relationship metamorphosizes. Yesterday, the same person was a role model, the next morning, the reverse, as he is despicable. This picture is practical and applies to everyone.

Above the table, on which an unpacked collection of sample cloth goods was spread out—Samsa was a traveling salesman—hung the picture which he had cut out of an illustrated magazine a little while ago and set in a pretty gilt frame [2].

Until he was a salesman, he was a Sisyphus. His profession continued until he converted to the insect. Even though he was unwilling to be a salesman, a family boulder, family debt, and Grete's violin education were on his head. He was ramming a boulder as much as he could. He was living in the underworld. No one respects his sacrifice after his termination.

"O God," he thought, "what a demanding job I've chosen! Day in, day out, on the road. The stresses of selling are much greater than the work going on at head office, and, in addition to that, I have to cope with the problems of travelling, the worries about train connections, irregular bad food, temporary and constantly changing human relationships which never come from the heart. To hell with it all" [3]!

He was bored, disturbed, and desperate within his job and work. He wanted to take a long vacation but his rock was a barrier. He had to push because he had many Hades and Thanatos in his life. He pushed himself and his boulder. He compared his work, travel, and food. He found hell, No Exit.

If I didn't hold back for my parent's sake, I'd have quit ages ago. I would've gone to the boss and told him just what I think from the bottom of my heart. He would've fallen right off his desk! How weird it is to sit up at that desk and talk down to the employee from way up there. The boss has trouble hearing, so the employee has to step up quite close to him. Anyway, I haven't completely given up that hope yet. Once I've got together the money to pay off my parents' debt to him—that should take another five or six years—I'll do it for sure. Then I'll make the big break. In any case, right now I have to get up. My train leaves at five o'clock [4]."

He wanted to take a long vacation. Under the giant rock, how can it be possible? He had to push his massive stone; otherwise, it could crush his family. So many things were on his mind, and he wanted to speak about them. While pushing a boulder it was impossible. First, he had to reach the mountain top.

"Gregor," a voice called—it was his mother!—"it's quarter to seven. Don't you want to be on your way?" However, as a result of the short conversation, the other family members became aware that Gregor was unexpectedly still at home, and already his father was knocking on one side door, weakly but with his fist. "Gregor, Gregor," he called out, "what's going on?" And, after a short while, he urged him on again in a deeper voice: "Gregor!" Gregor!" At the other side door, however, his sister knocked lightly. "Gregor? Are you all right? Do you need anything" [5]?

How lovely, respectful, humble, and polite greetings were. Mrs. Samsa and Grete were very close to him because he was a gold laying hen. We have a proverb about a hen with a golden egg. Whence a hen lays a golden egg, the hen is lovely for everyone. Love will terminate while stopping to lay the golden egg. Gregor was similar to a hen. It witnesses that the cause of love was not a hen, a golden egg.

She'd probably just gotten up out of bed now and hadn't even started to get dressed yet. Then why was she crying? Because he wasn't getting up and wasn't letting the manager in, because he was in danger of losing his position, and because then his boss would badger his parents once again with the old demands [6]?

Danger of losing a job is the cause of Grete's crying. The central point of the Novella is a job. Relation, respect, morality, love, and behavior are based on it. So, everyone fears that he might lose his position. Job means salary. Lack of pay calls several Pandoras. Income is an umbrella and fence, it covers all crises.

The manager must be held back, calmed down, convinced, and finally won over. The future of Gregor and his family really depended on it [7]!

The future of any employee and his family depends on employment. The working environment and employer are important.

In their condition, Gregor, and his family depended on him. His work was his hope and it helped to save them from a sinking boat. They were in terror that if the manager was not convinced consequences would be a wreck situation.

Those had been beautiful days, and they had never come back afterwards, at least not with the same splendour, in spite of the fact that Gregor later earned so much money that he was in a position to bear the expenses of the entire family, costs which he, in fact, did bear [8].

Onward to his destination, he was doing Bhageeratha effort. He wanted to take a rest once he touched the peak. He didn't arrive at the mountain top. He had continuously pushed his freight. It represents the employees of the world. A good salary is the source of our splendour life.

Part two

In part two, a form of Gregor is in the vermin. He can hear the conversation but cannot answer them. The body metamorphoses the insect, nevertheless, he wanted to do something for his poor family.

The language of his heart is kind. But kindness cannot feed the stomach. Everyone wants to listen, stomach language. He is sad; cannot do anything. Together with body transformation, his family and the world transformed in different shapes and behaviours.

He was not pitiful for his metamorphizes, he wanted to cry about the treatment from his family members. At the roar of the stomach, how father, mother, and Grete converted proletariat Sisyphus. We can see the fear Sisyphus forms in this part.

She walked to the side, caught sight of the enormous brown splotch on the flowered wallpaper, and, before she became truly aware that what she was looking at was Gregor, screamed out in a high pitched raw voice "Oh God, oh God" and fell with outstretched arms, as if she was surrendering everything, down onto the couch and lay there motionless. "Gregor, you... " cried out his sister with a raised fist and an urgent glare [9].

When Mrs. Samsa saw his metamorphic body, she was shocked and afraid. She was laid motionless. How horrible the situation was.

Abruptly, when we see insects or animals, the first reaction is fear. Though he was his son. Suppose, a member of the family, died, after his death, we fear that maybe he appears in the dark. If we see the same person, we terrorize because we think, that is his metaphoric ghost.

And should his old mother now perhaps work for money, a woman who suffered from asthma, for whom wandering through the apartment even now was a great strain and who spent every second day on the sofa by the open window labouring for breath [10]?

While her son earned, she didn't work. Now, she started to work. Agitation was the cause of her work. She had worried about how to maintain expenses if not working. She was aged Sisyphus transformed to proletariat because the massive rock was on the head.

But now he was standing up really straight, dressed in a tight-fitting blue uniform with gold buttons, like the ones servants wear in a banking company. Above the high stiff collar of his jacket his firm double chin stuck out prominently, beneath his bushy eyebrows the glance of his black eyes was freshly penetrating and alert, his otherwise dishevelled white hair was combed down into a carefully exact shining part. He threw his cap, on which a gold monogram, apparently the symbol of the bank, was affixed, in an arc across the entire room onto the sofa and moved, throwing back the edge of the long coat of his uniform, with his hands in his trouser pockets and a grim face, right up to Gregor [11].

Mr. Samsa started to work after Gregor's transformation. He was standing up really straight, dressed in a tight-fitting blue uniform with gold buttons, a high stiff collar of his jacket, white hair combed, threw cap, long coat of his uniform, these sprinkles were for offering himself to be a scapegoat. Due to work nature, employee decorates just like different Gods accept various animals. He dressed like a bank employee. He offered his candidacy (self-made scapegoat) to employers and customers.

It was an apple. Immediately a second one flew after it. Gregor stood still in fright. Further running away was useless, for his father had decided to bombard him [12].

Gregor was in fright because his father was in the mood to bombard him with apples. He wanted to escape as Sisyphus did once, but it was impossible. Albeit he was afraid, continuously bombarded apples and hurt him. His father was behaving to him like an enemy of the house.

Gregor's serious wound, from which he suffered for over a month—since no one ventured to remove the apple, it remained in his flesh as a visible reminder—seemed by itself to have reminded the father that, in spite of his present unhappy and hateful appearance, Gregor was a member of the family, something one should not treat as an enemy, and that it was, on the contrary, a requirement of family duty to suppress one's aversion and to endure—nothing else, just endure [13].

He was a loyal and humble son and brother. He always felt a responsibility, duty, and sincerity for the family. They were doing the same until he worked. On the contrary now, they behaved like the enemy and hated him. He endured all these —nothing else, just endure. His mind was the same only his body metamorphosed. In contrast, members of the family body didn't metamorphose but their behaviour metamorphoses. The reason was his income. Even if he had income, they might remain the same. In society, we can see many people get good care because of their assets. Those who have no assets or income, their children take them to an old age home. Gregor's serious wound, from which he suffered for over a month, no one cared for him. It is satire and sad for humanity.

Bent far over, the mother sewed fine undergarments for a fashion shop. The sister, who had taken on a job as a salesgirl, in the evening studied stenography and French, so as perhaps later to obtain a better position [14].

Until Gregor was a donkey, no one from his family, was ready to pull the cart off. When he was unable to pull the cart off, everyone started to pull. Everyone was unjust to him. At the time of his feeble and pitiable condition, they showed their irritation. Regarding the selfish human being, it is the overt example. Sister was getting ready to be a self-made scapegoat. Her study of stenography and French were plus points.

It even happened that various pieces of family jewellery, which previously the mother and sister had been overjoyed to wear on social and 35 festive occasions, were sold, as Gregor found out in the evening from the general discussion of the prices they had fetched [15].

In a normal situation, people enjoy, wear jewels, and have fun. At critical times they sell their items and property. In the end, they sell family members and self. We read before about a Roman slave, a man who sold his wife and child. Why? Because he wanted a secure life. Bad situations did not appeared in the Samsa family as severe as Roman slaves, so they sold merely ornaments to maintain family subsistence.

Gregor spent his nights and days with hardly any sleep. Sometimes he thought that the next time the door opened he would take over the family arrangements just as he had earlier [16].

How kind Gregor was, even wounded. In hard times, days and nights, he remembered his family. Still, he wanted to take over the family arrangements. Samsa's family should be proud of him, on the contrary, they ignored his all contributions.

At first, she also called him to her with words which she presumably thought were friendly, like "Come here for a bit, old dung beetle!" or "Hey, look at the old dung beetle" [17]!

How rude Grete's language was. Before his metamorphoses, she was so sweet and dearest to him. Now, she became the cruelest to him. We see how people metamorphosize under certain conditions.

People had grown accustomed to put into storage in his room things which they couldn't put anywhere else, and at this point there were many such things, now that they had rented one room of the apartment to three lodgers [18].

They sold themselves, they sold jewels and they rented rooms for their maintenance. Its reason was the survival crisis. If they didn't have a fear of crisis, it didn't require gradually more sales.

I immediately cancel my room. I will, of course, pay nothing at all for the days which I have lived here; on the contrary I shall think about whether or not I will initiate some sort of action against you, something which—believe me—will be very easy to establish." In fact, his two friends immediately joined in with their opinions, "We also give immediate notice [19]".

For income purposes, Samsa family rented their room but suddenly lodgers cancelled. What reason they did it, but blamed Gregor because he became a novelee (Novelee is the simplest term to replace the character. I use this term for my convenience.) of hate. He was being a scapegoat between his family and lodgers. Was it his fault? No, but he became a victim. It is a Kafkaesque. Kafkaesque is a scapegoat in another term because, without any crime, they became a victim. In Kafka's life, Hermann Kafka scapegoated him when he was 9 years old. Father's nature, beliefs, and habits made him a scapegoat. This accident was deeply rooted in his child's mind. It is revealed in his writing. Kafkaesque needs to be reread from a scapegoat perspective. Not only Gregor Samsa, Joseph K., and Georg Bendemann also became the scapegoat. The hierarchy of fear is in Kafkaesque. Those who have power cannot be scapegoated. Gregor Samsa, Joseph K., and Georg Bendemann were scapegoated by dignity, ego, prestige, power, and belief. Previously we read it from a Kafkaesque view.

Now we have scapegoat speculation. Kafkaesque belongs to the scapegoat family. When the father scapegoated the child, there are more invisible scapegoats. At the office, while employees scapegoated public, customers become invisible scapegoats. For example, in office delays work because of the supremacy of power, torture, harassment, and Kafkaesque. First, it makes scapegoats for Kafkas second, for the customer. In Kafkaesque, only first-hand Kafka is mentioned, invisible victims were (Droste scapegoats) ignored. A large number of such invisible scapegoats are in developing and under-developing countries. The office staff doesn't serve them in the best way. Even Kafka's designation harasses them.

"We must try to get rid of it," the sister now said decisively to the father, for the mother, in her coughing fit, was not listening to anything. "It is killing you both. I see it coming. When people have to work as hard as we all do, they cannot also tolerate this endless torment at home. I just can't go on anymore." "Child," said the father sympathetically and with obvious appreciation, "then what should we do?" "If only he understood us," said the father in a semi-questioning tone. The sister, in the midst of her sobbing, shook her hand energetically as a sign that there was no point thinking of that. "If he only understood us," repeated the father and by shutting his eyes he absorbed the sister's conviction of the impossibility of this point, "then perhaps some compromise would be possible with him. But as it is… [20]"

Let's see an instance. Family members are making scapegoats for Gregor for all their bad fortune. He was innocent. Neither he made a mistake nor he did the crime but they were fired up with resentment and blamed him because he was feeble. Physically, and economically he was weak. In this wretch situation, all blame he had to endure.

Yet, neither he answered nor spoke against them. He was always loyal to his family. He represents the marginal, subaltern, female, transgender, refugee, migrant, and untouchable. Society used SSS to make them a scapegoat. Joseph K., Georg Bendemann, and Gregor are not mere characters of Kafkaesque; they are characters of scapegoats too. We have many such scapegoats in family and society.

"It must be gotten rid of," cried the sister. "That is the only way, father. You must try to get rid of the idea that this is Gregor. The fact that we have believed for so long, that is truly our real misfortune. But how can it be Gregor? If it were Gregor, he would have long ago realized that a communal life among human beings is not possible with such an animal and would have gone away voluntarily. Then we would not have a brother, but we could go on living and honour his memory. But this animal plagues us. It drives away the lodgers, will obviously take over the entire apartment, and leave us to spend the night in the alley" [21].

Every action, shout, and language, Grete tried to show her brother as despicable, hateful, and marginal. She couldn't do it when he was strong and had remuneration. If any accident happens in a family, its vice goes to those who are weak. We have more of a fearological question than the philosophical question of Camus. This question was not answered by any philosopher. Were Gregor, Joseph K., and Georg Bendemann not scapegoated? My answer is they were scapegoated by family, society, and the nation.

"What now?" Gregor asked himself and looked around him in the darkness. He soon made the discovery that he could no longer move at all. He was not surprised at that. On the contrary, it struck him as unnatural that up to this point he had really been able up to move around with these thin little legs. Besides, he felt relatively content. True, he had pains throughout his entire body, but it seemed to him that they were gradually becoming weaker and weaker and would finally go away completely.

The rotten apple in his back and the inflamed surrounding area, entirely covered with white dust, he hardly noticed. He remembered his family with deep feelings of love. In this business, his own thought that he had to disappear was, if possible, even more decisive than his sister's. He remained in this state of empty and peaceful reflection until the tower clock struck three o'clock in the morning.

From the window he witnessed the beginning of the general dawning outside. Then without willing it, his head sank all the way down, and from his nostrils flowed out weakly his last breath [22].

At the end, Gregor from his nostrils flowed out weakly his last breath. It is the pitiable death of Gregor; another term is suicide and mental murder. Most of Kafka's novelee die, commit suicide, and kill. They are not self-scapegoated, they are made so by family, society, and nation. In Sartre's language, 'hell is other people'. Yes, a hell of them is made by other people.

From this standpoint, we can see the life of Gregor, Joseph K., and Georg Bendemann (Kafkaesque). Kafkaesque can be studied from multiple dimensions like hell is other people, scapegoat, and Sisyphus. As said by Ashley Crossman they had been unfairly blamed. After the punishment, Kafka became 'yes Sisyphus' in front of his father because he feared that if he did not listen to him, he will give the massive rock to push up the mountain, to the top as the cold weather of Prague. This fear made him fear Sisyphus and his whole life he pushed a boulder of fear. He applied it in the books and Kafkaesque theories.

The same case is in *The Judgment*. Georg Bendemann's father said pityingly, in an offhand manner: "I suppose you wanted to say that sooner. But now it doesn't matter." And in a louder voice: "So now you know what else there was in the world besides yourself, till now you've known only about yourself! An innocent child, yes, that you were, truly, but still more truly have you been a devilish human being! - And therefore take note: I sentence you now to death by drowning [23]!" When Joseph K., Georg Bendemann and Gregor were scapegoated, all the family members became invisibly scapegoated too. Invisible Scapegoat has second, third, fourth, and more victims. Georg was innocent though his father unfairly charged and compelled him to drown.

It has three layers: (1) Body metamorphosis (sick, mad, disabled, handicapped, old age, termination from the job, loss in business, retirement), (2) Financial Metamorphosis, (3) Fearmorphosis.

In other words: 1. Metamorphosis of finance, 2. Metamorphosis of beliefs, 3. Metamorphosis of fear.

At the time of sleep, a man is a student, unemployed, next day when he wakes up, he finds himself vermin employee. All living creatures transform into different professions. Sometimes a man makes a man vermin as other people are hell. When we see a crowd of people from the sky, they look like vermin.

End Notes

1. Kafka (1912), p. 1.
2. Ibid., p. 2.
3. Ibid., p. 3-4.
4. Ibid., p. 4.

5. Ibid., p. 5.
6. Ibid., p. 9.
7. Ibid., p. 14.
8. Ibid., p. 23.
9. Ibid., p. 30.
10. Ibid., p. 24.
11. Ibid., p. 32.
12. Ibid.
13. Ibid., p. 34.
14. Ibid.
15. Ibid., p. 35-6.
16. Ibid., p. 36.
17. Ibid., p. 38.
18. Ibid.
19. Ibid., p. 42.
20. Ibid., p. 43.
21. Ibid., p. 44.
22. Ibid., p. 45.
23. http://franzkafkastories.com/shortStories.php?story_id=kafka_the_
    judgement

REFERENCES

Adhikari, B. S. (2020). *Yarshagumbaism*. Xlibris.

Adhikari, B. S., Kalu, O. A., and Subba, D. (2020). *Eco-Fearism prospects and burning issues*. Xlibris.

Camus, A.. (1955). *The myth of Sisyphus and other essays*. Vintage Books.

Derrida, J. (1976). *Of grammatology* (trans. by G. C. Spivak). John Hopkins University Press.

Dharabasi, K. (2017). *LEELABOTH*. Pairavi Book House.

Fisher, R. M. (2022). *Philosophy of fearism: A primer*. Xlibris.

Fisher, R. M. (2017). Eco-Philosophy of fearism and ecocriticism: In an Age of Terror. Technical Paper No. 68. In Search of Fearlessness Research Institute.

Homer. (n.d.). *The Odyssey*. Book X1. Chapman's Homer.

Johansen, K. R. (2021). Fearism. https://www.academia.edu/82040476/Fearism

Kafka, F. (1912). *The metamorphosis* (Translator: Ian Johnston). Feedbooks. file:///Users/limbunisham/Downloads/Franz_Kafka_The_Met amorphosis.pdf

Kalu, O. A. (2017). *The first stage of the fearologist*. Self- published

King, P. (2019). Albert Camus and the problem of absurdity. https://blog.oup. com/2019/05/albert-camus-problem-absurdity/

Kumar, B. M., and Sushmita, B. S. (2018). *The youth don't cry*. Indra Publishing House.

Mahajan, C. P. (2020). Of animals of sacrifice. https://hillpost.in/2020/09/ of-animals-of-sacrifice/114598/

Marx, K. (1998/2021). *Das Kapital.*. Pvt. Ltd. Vol. I, II, III. Prakash Books, India

Marx, K., and Engels, F. (2015). *Communist Manifesto*. St. Martin Press.

Rai, D. S. (B.S. 2069). *Garima Monthly Magazine*, 364.

Subba, Desh (interviewed by Adhikari, Bishwa Raj). (2021a). An interview with Desh Subba on 'Trans Philosophism.' *Livemandu*. https://livemandu.com/ archives/27019

Subba, Desh. (2021b). *Trans philosophism: Trans philosophism doctrine on Marxism, postmodernism, existentialism, criticism, sociology, ecology, politics, science and language.* Xlibris.

Subba, Desh. (2014). *Philosophy of fearism: Life is conducted, directed and controlled by the fear.* Xlibris.

INDEX

Manufactured by Amazon.ca
Acheson, AB

14602487R00118